Arour
Rushton

Rushton Mill & Cloud End.

Compiled by Sheila Hine

Frontcover: Rogers family
Back: Roadmen at the Fox and Rushton Mill in the 1930s.

CHURNET VALLEY BOOKS
1 King Street, Leek, Staffordshire. ST13 5NW 01538 399033
www.leekbooks.co.uk
© Sheila Hine and Churnet Valley Books 2005
Most of the photographs and illustrations in this book
are the personal property of local people and are copyright

ISBN 1 904546 28 5

This is believed to be the local Yeomanry, outside the Robin Hood in Rushton. Horses were brought from Canada during WWI for stabling and training in the field to the right of the inn, before going out to the front.

THE RUSHTONS.

RUSHTON SPENCER, a small village on an acclivity within a short distance of the Leek and Macclesfield turnpike road, and near the station on the Churnet Valley railway, which passes through this township, is 157 miles from London, 7 from Macclesfield, 63½ from Leeds, 26 from Manchester, 43½ from Derby, and 5 north-west from Leek, in the parochial chapelry of Rushton (which includes the three townships of Rushton Spencer, Rushton James, and Heaton, and the hamlet of Rushton Marsh), North Totmonslow hundred, Leek union and county court district, Lichfield diocese, Stafford archdeaconry, and Leek deanery, North Staffordshire. The living is a perpetual curacy, annual value £110, held by the Rev. William Melland, and in the gift of the vicar of Leek. The chapel is a small ancient and curious structure, and has 1 bell. The chapel is supposed by some to have been founded before Leek, and was anciently called "The chapel in the wilderness." There is also a Wesleyan Methodist chapel. The poor of Rushton Spencer have the following benefactions :—A house and 1½ acre of land, let for £7 per annum, purchased in 1753, with £23 left by Alice Yeardley and Mary Sidebottom ; the rent is chiefly distributed in weekly doles of bread. The manor of Rushton Spencer, which formerly belonged to the De Spencer, Savage, and other families, now belongs to the freeholders. The population in 1851 was 355.

RUSHTON MARSH, within Rushton Spencer, is a hamlet close to the turnpike road. Here is a Free school, built by subscription in 1772, endowed with land worth £3 per annum.

RUSHTON JAMES, a hamlet and township, distant 5 miles north-west of Leek, in the manor of Horton ; the acreage is 1,000; population in 1851, 283. Gibbs Crawford Antrobus, Esq., is lord of the manor. The poor have the following annual sum :—In 1725, Elizabeth Hulme left the yearly sum of £4 out of her messuage at Woodehouse Green, to be distributed in clothing on October 16th.

Rushton Spencer.

PRIVATE RESIDENTS.

Meir Henry, esq. Bridestones
Melland Rev. William [incumbent], Parsonage
Simpson Miles, esq. Lee house
Yardley Mr. Thomas

COMMERCIAL.

Bailey Josiah, farmer, Woodhouse grn
Boon William, farmer, Cloud side
Bradburn Samuel, shopkeeper
Buxton Nathan, farmer
Chappell John, *Golden Lion*
Chappell Nathan, farmer, Tofts green
Chappell Thomas, assistant overseer
Cook James, silk dyer
Goodwin Ann (Mrs.), farmer, Lymnford
Hulme Amos, farmer, Woodhouse grn
Hunt Charles, farmer, Cloud side
Jerrard John, shoemaker
Kennerley John, farmer, Cloud side
Kent George, *Robin Hood*
Knight Thomas, farmer, Cloud side
Knight Thomas, shoemaker
Lockitt George, farmer, Hall house
Lockitt John, farmer, High Lee
Longden Mathias, *Hanging Gate*, joiner
Moulton Wm. farmer, Woodhouse green
Myatt Samuel, *Royal Oak*, Rushton marsh
Nixon Thomas, farmer, Marsh side
Procter Hannah (Mrs.), farmer, Oulton
Rigby Joseph, blacksmith
Sunner Simon Myatt, farmer, Bank
Tomkinson Wm. farmer, Lane end
Vernon Hannah Mrs, *Rushton Railway inn*
Vernon John, farmer, Raven's clough
Whittaker Thomas, miller, Rushton mill
Willshaw George, shopkeeper
Wood James, farmer, Sand bank
Wright Wm. farmer, Cloud house
Yardley John Plant, farmer, Wall hill
Yates Henry, farmer, Nether lee
Letters received through Leek

Rushton James.

Bostock Rev. James, M.A. [incumbent of Wincle, Cheshire], Wolfdale

COMMERCIAL.

Armitt Mary (Mrs.), farmer
Bailey Moses & Isaac, wheelwr'ts Wolf Low
Bailey John, farmer, Rushton hall
Boon Thomas, farmer, Harpers
Bradley Thomas, farmer, Dingle
Buxton Samuel, farmer, Rushton hall
Buxton Thos. jun. farmer, Old Crown
Clowes John, farmer, Ox Hay
Condliffe Thomas, farmer, Hayes
Dale Charles, blacksmith
Dale Wm. farmer, Rycroft gate
Doorbar Enoch, farmer, Stoney edge
Gibson Enoch, farmer, Endon ease
Gibson Thomas, *Fox*, & rake maker
Knight John, farmer, New town
Knight John, farmer, Wolfdale hay
Knight William, farmer, Long edge end
Lockett Thomas, farmer
Pass Simeon, farmer
Rowley James, farmer, Ashmore house
Shufflebotham Joseph, farmer, Lee
Winkle William, *Crown*, & blacksmith
Letters through Leek

Free School, Henry James Mayer, master ; Mrs. Sarah Ann Mayer, mistress
Railway Station, George Goldsmith, station master

Rushton from the Kelly's Directory of 1863.

CONTENTS

Acknowledgements

My thanks to everyone who has helped in any way, contributing their memories or their photographs, or giving me encouragement.
Thanks to Karen Cope, Ann Dowley, Margaret Russell, Josie Hambleton, Cynthia Jones and Glenys Terry for the use of their notes.
And special thanks to Susan Davis for her proof-reading.

The May Queen about 1920.

Miss Simpson's class, about 1933
Back: Leslie Goodwin, John Davies, - -, Derek Trueman, Stanley Malkin, Arthur Woodward, - -
2nd row: Una Cantrill, Nancy Wood, Nancy Warburton, Freda Gibson, Muriel Malkin, Virgenie Cantrill
3rd row: Dorothy Knight, Dorothy Brassington, Mona Moss, Phyllis Beech, Marjorie Harrison, Dorothy Wood,
Gwen Birley, Margaret Bowyer.   Front: Peter Robinson, Philip Gibson, - -, - -

Una Hadfield

I was born on March 23rd, 1925 at Marsh View, Rushton Spencer, the home of my grandparents, Mary and James Goodfellow. My parents were due to move house on March 25th from their first home at Longsdon to Wall Hill Cottage at Rushton, where we lived for the next 7 years. There was a field and outbuildings adjoining the cottage and my father carried on his cattle dealing business from there. The cottage is situated just behind the Feeder, which takes water from the River Dane to Rudyard Lake, a distance of about three miles.

Of course the inevitable happened when my sister Virgenie and I were supposed to be playing in the garden. We went down to the bridge about 100yds away and pretended to be fishing with our skipping ropes. I fell in; I was almost 6 years old and my sister would be just eight. She knew that dad was out and that mother was looking after our sister Edith, who was 15 months old. The Feeder was in flood; it was February and thawing after a heavy snow. I was swept along quickly, so my sister ran to Lane End Farm alongside the canal to George Malkin, who was milking his cows at the time. Luckily for me, he knew that she was not joking and although he couldn't swim, he got me out.

Mrs Malkin took me home and scolded me all the way. All I was worried about was that I'd lost one of my Wellingtons. Soon afterwards, we moved to New House Farm on the other side of the village, where we lived for the next 12 years.

I didn't want to leave school at 14, but that was the rule and I was needed at home. I was 14 and left school at Easter 1939 to help look after my sisters, Edith, 9, and Elizabeth, 6, and also help with cooking and cleaning, looking after the animals and harvesting. Mother enrolled me for evening classes in maths and English. War was declared and she was asked to be Billeting Officer for evacuees to be sent from Manchester. Every household had to be checked for bedroom space and forms galore had to be filled in.

The children were often homesick and unhappy. Later on we had twenty boys from London and all but two were taken into families; the last two had to come home with us and stayed for around twelve months.

At that time, we had no electricity and only one cold water tap in the house, on the back kitchen sink; the water was pumped from a spring below a steep bank, by a temperamental hydraulic ram housed in a concrete bunker and driven by the brook which flowed through three of our fields. We had a black fire-grate in the living room, the coal fire in the centre with an oven on one side and a boiler on the other, the only means of heating water apart from kettles and pans, which stood on the fire and were blackened.

Having no electricity was the worst thing, we only had candles and oil lamps and a storm lantern for outside. Paraffin had to be fetched nearly every night in the winter, in a gallon can, from the Hanging Gate pub.

Una and Virgenie.

The ironing was a rotten job, as the irons had to be heated on the fire, taken off with great care, and cleaned before they could be used. We had a wonderful mother's help called Alice, she came when Elizabeth was born and lived in for a month. After that she came every Wednesday to do washing and ironing - with copper and mangle in those days - and every Saturday to do some cleaning.

Father had a man called Bill to do the milking and general farm work, looking after the cattle, pigs and a few sheep. We had a very good collie, Floss, who knew instinctively what to do when driving cattle to Leek from Rushton on Wednesday market day. There were few cars on the road then. Once a month, dad went to Flash auction; we went with him in holidays. He went to Banbury every Thursday - the cattle were delivered on Friday morning - and he went to Northampton on Saturdays; the cattle coming on the Sunday.

When the train came in to the station, they were unloaded into a pen and the Stationmaster would phone to say, *"Your cattle have arrived"*. We had to shut all the garden gates on the way down the Marsh. Dad drove the car and sometimes we rode on the running board with a stick, one on each side and the dog sending them on. On a Sunday morning, we fetched them before Chapel unless they arrived late, when we dreaded meeting folks going to Chapel all dressed up and we were in our 'rough'.

At Mrs Turnock's bakery, there would be at least three girls serving their apprenticeship at any one time. During one very bad winter, when the roads were completely blocked with snow, they couldn't bake the bread needed for the village, as they had no yeast. Our dad went to Leek on horseback through the drifts, for two large bags of yeast in very closely woven sacking. It was a perilous journey. Although there was the LMS railway (London, Midland and Scottish) the trains were also out of action.

Until the mid-1930s a well-dressing was held in the village every year. We school children were allowed to vote for the girl to be the May Queen; then after school for many weeks, we had to rehearse the country and maypole dances. During the Whit week's holiday, a large frame was carried into the school and covered in clay. All the villagers brought flowers to be pressed into the clay to make designs and pictures. When finished, it was taken to Daniel's well on the Leek Old Road. This reportedly only ran dry to precede a national calamity, like the first war.

On the day of the celebrations, the Queen was carried shoulder-high in a basket type chair, from the school to the well, by the Parish Councillors and school governors; of which my grandfather, James Goodfellow was one. The vicar, Rev Herbert Smith held a short service, the Queen was given a glass of water from the well and all then proceeded back to the school grounds for maypole dancing, refreshments and games.

As it was a C of E school, the vicar was a regular visitor. On St George's Day and Armistice Day, we all marched up to the Church through the fields for a service. The

Methodist ministers were never included in these activities as they would perhaps be these days. Once a week, the girls had a sewing class with Miss Goldstraw; the boys did woodwork in winter and gardening in summer.

What is now Horseshoe Cottage was the Post Office, kept by Postmistress, Sally Cook and incorporating a very small telephone exchange, serving about eight subscribers until just before the war, when twenty more people were wired up. There were four postmen and one postwoman; Mr Jack Allen, Mr Charles Goodwin, Mr Tom Cundiff, Mr George Hulse and Miss Fanny Cave. Two of the postmen had been wounded in the first war and had only one arm, but they still managed to sort and deliver the mail, walking great distances, six days every week. The mail going outwards from the letter boxes was collected on the postmen's return journey, put into a bag, tied up with a label marked Macclesfield, sealed with sealing wax and taken to the six o'clock train.

Our family were Methodists and we all attended the chapel Sunday school. The teachers were Mr James Needham and Mr John Needham for the boys and Mrs Lydia Hine and Miss Ethel Needham for the girls. There would be about 40 pupils. On the first Sunday in August the Anniversary was held, when the children sang at morning and evening services to a packed congregation.

On the two previous Sundays, the children, accompanied by the band walked to most of the houses in the village and around, singing a hymn at each house and inviting the occupants to the Anniversary. On the first Sunday morning, we would go as far as Rushton James, then back to the chapel schoolrooms where a meal was laid on. Afterwards we took the road to Heaton, where some wag suggested we should sing the hymn 'Sound the Battle Cry' as there was a long-standing dispute between two lady residents in the village of Heaton. On the second Sunday, we started at The Marsh, taking in Station Lane and The Anthony, then to the Golden Lion, then through a stile, over the railway to John Cook's and along to the Lea Farm, where we turned back along Mill lane to the Miss Cave's home, where we had herb beer made with Mason's Extract and biscuits. The long tradition of Walking Sundays had to be discontinued around the mid-1970s, owing to the increasing traffic.

During Christmas week, the chapel members produced a concert, at which the children and adults recited poems and sang various pieces, with piano and organ recitals. The following afternoon and evening, the Sunday school children had a party organised for them with lovely refreshments and a large decorated tree. Every child was presented with a book prize.

In the summer holidays in August, a Sunday school trip was organised to the seaside; Blackpool, Southport or Rhyl were the usual places. Mother usually went with us and one year, when dad also went, he took us up in an aeroplane, a De-Havilland; a great thrill, which I have never forgotten.

Woodwork and gardening class, 1914/15.

At the station, station staff and postmen.
Mr Jefferies, stationmaster, centre.
Wilfrid Gibson, back row 3rd from left.

Chapel fundraising event 1930s

Mr Harrison, Mr H.Harrison, Mr Keen, Mrs Robinson, John Needham, Minnie Buckley

Mr J. Needham, Fanny Cave, Hilda Keen, Ethel Needham, Mary Eardley, Mrs Cantrill, Mrs Harrison, Mr Blakemore, Mrs Moss, Ivy Dale

Front: Mrs Hine, Mrs Keen, Jessie Moss, Mrs Gilbert, Revd Withers, Dorothy Davis, Edith Cantrill, Mrs Mellor, Mrs T. Massey, Mr T. Massey.

RUSHTON VILLAGE.

Rushton, NSR.

Arthur Chappell

R.K. Robinson, known as Dickie, from Manchester, bought the field bordering Station Lane in the mid-1920s. He built a bungalow, now replaced with a traditional house, and imported a London coffee stall and put it behind the wall, fronting the main road. Another couple from Manchester, named Batty, came and lodged at Marsh Villa. They ran this stall on wheels for quite a while, serving passing wagons and motors, which were increasing. Dickie and his son Frank built the transport café and the garage, which had petrol pumps. It was a hive of industry through the war. Wainwright's lads from Mare Knowles, up at Wincle, used to bring scores and scores of rabbits and sell them to the wagon drivers.

Mr and Mrs Preston built a shop along the Marsh in the early thirties. On Friday nights, the Weekly Sentinel came in, which was the paper most people had with all the local news in. All the youths used to come and collect them. There'd be 30 or 40 and it 'ud be who'd got the best bike or the fastest bike. It could get a bit lively. The policeman lived next door, Mr Davenport, later Mr Hartell. He'd come round and sit with the lads. He knew what was going on and had our respect. Some of the lads would sit on the Oak bridge before going down to the shop. One or two liked a drop of beer. There was an Irish lad, Paddy, who worked at Fairboroughs. Jim Bailey bet him that he couldn't drink 8 pints in 10 minutes. It was the price of the beer plus 10 bob, and he won it.

I started school in 1925 - Billy Banks retired in 1926 and his son Harold took over. The school regime was strict but happy. The old cane came out, but he got results. There were some rough lads, because they were rough times, but they all made out, not a one fallen by the wayside.

In 1933, we were sent home on 27th January because there was a blizzard blowing and it blocked everywhere, on the Friday. The railway didn't come through until Monday. We'd started sending milk by road then and the road didn't run for a fortnight. It repeated itself on the same day in 1947 and they finally ridded Long Edge out, all by hand in those days, on the 25th of March.

I started work for Bob Robinson, up Sugar Street, when I left school. It was Boxing Day 1935, half a crown a week. That first week we had to sharpen all the tools from the school workshop. I was busy turning the grindstone. The winters were harder then and men were laid off. So Bob said, *"Stand down next week"*. So I went helping Uncle Jim Turnock shift his shed at Alley House. Bob was across the road and said, *"What are you doing here, I thought you worked for me?"* *"Well, you said there was nowt to do."* Then he said, *"Be back next Monday and I'll give you 5 bob a week."*

I had to milk a few cows first thing, then get to work for ten to eight. The first job at work was to fetch water, either from Daniel's well or Bella well. We finished at 5.30, but that meant when the twenty to six train came up. It was the same on Saturday; we finished at half past twelve, when the quarter to one train came!

Robinsons was chiefly wheelwrights in those days. They used to bring vehicles down from Swythamley area, Wildboarclough, Leek, Biddulph Park. Farm wagons, carts, milk floats through to gigs and traps. All had wooden wheels with iron hoops and the traps had a groove in theirs, which you sprung a rubber tyre onto. There was some very nice work done, the traps and floats were painted up, varnished, lined out and named. The best traps had hickory shafts, which bent like springs, capped off at the end with brass, then patent leather back 22 inches to the saddle clips. We made everything to do with vehicles; it would take a signwriter a full day to line and letter a unit. Later on when pneumatic tyres and tractors came in and people would pull anything - all that vanished.

Wheelwrighting was very interesting, making the wooden wheels. The staves and spokes were made from oak and the felloes from ash or elm. You'd get all those done, then hoop a dozen or more in one session. You matched the wheels to the hoops, which were $1^{1}/2$ inches less than the circumference of the wheel. When they were put on hot, they expanded and then when they cooled they contracted and pulled the wheel tight together. If the hoops were pretty good, we re-used them - otherwise we got a new one. Careys at Manchester were the chief suppliers. And every wheelwright had a blacksmith's shop, so a lot of iron work could be dealt with.

In the morning on hooping day, you'd get the hoops ready and number them to the wheels. Then set them up in a stack with bits in between, smaller ones on the inside, bigger ones to the outside. All the old timber that you'd taken off the old carts and what not had been cut up, so you stacked that round and lit it all up. Then you went for lunch and after about half an hour they were ready. Then all hell was let loose. Once you disturbed the fire, you'd got to work fast; there'd be three of us, maybe four. You put the wheel down on a face-plate and tightened it down. Then one chap would lift the front edge of the hoop up with his hooping tool and the two other men were able to slide a long iron bar under the centre and carry it to the face plate and drop it over the wheel. Then some buckets of water over it, release it from the plate, rear it up, put a rod through the bush and drop it onto a trestle, so that it could be spun through a trough of water. It was all done in a matter of minutes. In about an hour, you'd got the lot done, and you were wet through, black as coal and jiggered up.

As time progressed, the pneumatic tyres came in; I was sorry to see it all go. We did joinery as well and undertaking. If one of those jobs came in, everything else had to stop, because there was no mortuary or embalming then. The coffin had to be pitched out and made waterproof. You had to melt the pitch and swill it all round the bottom and so far up the sides. Old Bob got dressed up with his top hat and there was a horse hearse.

We made yokes, usually out of elderberry for lightness; and cambrells for

One of my carts at Wormhill.

pig-killing out of ash. We cut our own native timber. You'd buy a tree from a farmer, cut it when the sap was down, saw it up and leave it to season. There was a fair old stack.

There was the 10 o'clock goods train. Everything came by rail; the timber for Robinsons, coal, cattle feed. Jim Arthur Gibson, from Ryecroft, used to do public waggoning with a horse, so he used to fetch for us from the station. And Moss and Lovatt or Bartram's, would perhaps fetch stuff up in the afternoons when they'd finished the milk. After the war we had a James three-wheeler pick-up truck. You straddled a tank like a motor bike and it had motor bike type handlebars and windscreen.

Old Bob packed up about 1940 and Edgar took over. He didn't like the undertaking and let it tail off; Arnold Turnock took the extra on. Then eventually, he finished, sold out and the workshop became a corn warehouse for Jim Goodfellow.

The village was self contained then, the railway was a big thing, 21 trains a day, plus goods trains. Nine employed at the station and three on the line. The ganger, Arthur Bailey, walked from Bosley to Rudyard every day; up one line and down the other, checking for loose cleats or anything wrong. The linesmen looked after the track and kept the sides tidy. Frank Condliffe and Jim Trueman were local.

In holiday time there were four excursion trains, the sidings were full of carriages. It was like Victoria Station when they came off the train. They went walking off to the Dane valley. The Brassingtons at Feeder Cottage made a fortune catering. When they left there, they set up as confectioners in Leek. Albert Trueman had a tearoom; Mrs Bartram used to cater, and The Anthony. You could come down on the train for about 1s 3d and have 2s 6d in your pocket and have a good day out. It fizzled out because after the war there was a different outlook.

The North Western buses used to run every odd hour up bank and every even hour down to Macclesfield, and the Manchester-Derby bus ran through three times a day. There's no public transport now to what there was; I think we've gone backwards.

When I came here, the rates were two shillings a week. We had a village bobby and there were three lengthsmen on the roads, Jack and Bill Armitt and Tom Cope.

We went to chapel Sunday school because it was closer. There was a service at church in the morning; the vicar did Swythamley at night. Old Vicar Smith was an MA and his salary then was equal to three times a tradesman's salary. He was the only one in Rushton who could afford a maid. He used to get £1 10s for doing Swythamley at night. He was on £10 or £12 a week and a tradesman would get about £3. Everyone looked up to the vicar and the headmaster.

There was a smithy here at Marsh Cottage, the Holland family were here, and I think all of them were born here. Then Mr Holland built the smithy down the road, but it got too much for him and shortly afterwards Mrs Holland found herself widowed. So she advertised for a blacksmith to run the smithy and Bill Bartram from Tutbury got the job. He ended up marrying Mrs Holland and became stepfather to the children. This was during the first war, so he and the Holland lads, after their normal work, at night turned thousands of horseshoes for the armed services. In the 1920s they started the haulage business (Bartram and Holland).

Ben Wilde lived at Pitt Slacks and had his garage on top. He took everything to

Rushton Methodist chapel

Meerbrook about 1937. I've pushed a handcart from Rushton over Gun to Meerbrook when we were working there many a time.

On a Saturday night we'd catch the ten to six train to Manchester, to go to Bellevue. It picked up all the way from Uttoxeter. We got to Longside station for 6.30 and it was 6d to get in. There was the zoo, speedway, dance hall, boxing sometimes and fireworks across the lake. We were back here for quarter to eleven. It closed in the late forties.

When I was working at Robinsons, we used to do a fair bit of work at the Fox. We went up one Monday morning, Hugh Barker and myself, to renew the bedroom floors. They had a woman worked for them, well she lived there, they never paid her, named Maria. We started and stripped the boards up and borrowed the sweeping brush to brush the joists off. Maria came up and she walked straight across the plaster ceiling. She just got hold of the brush and through she went onto the bar!

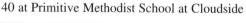

1851 SUNDAY SCHOOL ATTENDANCE CENSUS

40 at C of E school
36 at Wesleyan Methodist School, Alley Lane
46 at Wesleyan Methodist School, Diglake (Marsh)
40 at Primitive Methodist School at Cloudside

Mr Jefferies, stationmaster.

RUSHTON SCHOOL 1926. Back row: Josh Knowles, Ernest Oliver, Norman Biddulph, Arthur Trueman, Charlie Bailey, Bill Goldstraw, Harold Tomkinson, Arthur Eardley, Arthur Allen, Arthur Teats, Clifford Dale, Thomas Meakin, Barry Bailey, Gilbert Chappell, Sid Bailey, Mr Banks

2nd: Miss Goldstraw, Joan Gibson, Nelly Eardley, Florrie Heapy, Mabel Chappell, Gertie Robinson, Dorothy Gibson, Connie Willbanks, Edith Bailey, Hilda Goodwin, Mary Jackson, Vera Bailey, Dorothy Cook, _ _, Jean Meakin, Marion Sheldon, Annie Foster, Marion Jacobs, Dorothy Scott, Miss Simpson.

3rd: Harriet Woodward, Vivien Foden, Millie Cheetham, Elsie Teats, Annie Bailey, Emily Goldstraw, Elsie Bailey, Hilda Bailey, - -, Annie Slaner, Edith Robinson, Gladys Bowyer, Eva Bailey, Mary Sheldon, Mary Wright, Phyllis Corbishley, Sarah Bailey.

4th: Frank Bailey, _ _, Dorothy Wood, Marjorie Boon, Nelly Bailey, _ _, Ruth Warburton, Elsie Wood, Marjorie Moss, Elsie Allen, Elsie Sutton, Annie Simpson, Eva Bailey, Virgenie Cantrill, Mona Moss, Mary Clulow, Gladys Gibson, Arthur Chappell, Stanley Malkin.

5th: Arthur Woodward, Kenneth Goodfellow, _ _, Ernest Robinson, Harry Bailey, Horace Knowles, - Clulow, Jim Cotterill, Tommy Cheetham, Victor Moss, Jim Bailey, Ernest Davies, Ronnie Goldstraw, Harry Wright, - -.

6th: - -, - -, Harry Wright, John Fletcher, Billy Gibson, Edgar Warburton, - -, Jack Cope, - -, - -, Philip Gibson, John Foster, Derek Trueman

Rushton School, early 1930s.

At the opening of Rushton chapel 1st June 1899.

IN FRONT OF RUSHTON VICARAGE.

Technical Instruction in Butter-making (Parish magazine March 1895)

We hope to call together soon a local committee to consider the desirability of applying to the County Council for courses of instruction in butter-making. A course of instruction may consist of five or ten lessons given on successive days. At each lesson from 12 to 16 pupils can receive practical instruction in the whole process of butter-making. The fees paid by the pupils will be 2/6 each, and for spectators , 6d or 3d each as the committee may decide.

Mary Dale

Aunty Lizzie Goodfellow had a confectioners shop on St Edward's Street in Leek, in the early 1900s. Aunty Rachel and mother went to help out there and that's where she met my father. He was a shoemaker at Salter and Salter's shoe shop next door. He was a widower of 49 and mother was 37. They got married in 1917 and went to live at Chapel House, Alley Lane in Rushton. It was also known as Woodlands; I was born there in 1918.

He started his shoe repairing business up there. He made a lot of clogs; I could nearly make a clog to this day, I used to tinker in the workshop with him. He bought the clog tops ready made and the wooden soles and assembled them, then putting on the brass toe caps and the clog irons underneath. A lot of men brought their boots in and had them made into clogs, *"Will you clog me these?"*

After a while, he had a shed in the little field opposite the Oak, where the path goes up to the church. It was more convenient for people to go there. Then we moved down to the Marsh and he moved the shed there and cobbled all day In summer, he got up very early to do the gardening because he was more interested in that than cobbling.

In those days, there were a lot of tramps used to walk through from Macclesfield to Leek, from one workhouse to the next. They had very poor footwear and one tells another and they used to call at dad's shop to see if he'd got any old boots or shoes to fit them. He always fitted them up with something; if he hadn't got anything, he'd codge something together for them.

He was a town man and when the farm men brought their boots in to be mended or clogged, they used to smell so vile of cow manure, he had an old bath outside and he used to just chuck them in it and let them soak for days until they smelled sweeter.

We had a little dog called Nip, a Manchester terrier. When we were up Alley Lane, Mr William Banks lived opposite and he used to say, *"That dog ought to have been a Punch and Judy dog"*, because we used to dress her up in doll's clothes and goodness knows what. Always in the summer holidays we used to have our own well dressing, because at the back of that house there is a well. The dog was always the queen, dressed up in a doll's dress, a garland round her neck and flowers. Then usually in the middle of it all, Nell Wright, who was a little black and white terrier, a little horror, she'd come tearing down from Wrights and Nip would give one look, jump out of the chair and off they'd go across the fields. Nip in this dress; you can imagine what she'd look like when she came back.

At school, Mr Harold Banks was a very good teacher. After I'd left, my father insisted that I went to night school in Leek for two years to do English, geography and arithmetic but apart from the arithmetic, which I never did like, I'd already learned it; Mr Banks had already covered it. Ken Goodfellow had the cane nearly every day, he was very mischievous. When he left school, Mr Banks gave him a small piece of it, which he'd cut off as a memento. Ken's father didn't see the funny side of it. Girls didn't usually have the cane, but Harriet Woodward had it for giggling.

Our one outing of the week was to go down to Goodfellow's shop to my Aunty Mary's with my mother to buy the week's groceries and that was quite a thing, to go there and see different people. This was mid-1920s, that was exciting to go and see life.

Looking down Station Lane.

The Robin Hood is on the left, the Royal Oak on the right.

Mrs Bartram had a shop too at the top of Station Lane; she used to keep open on a Sunday and that was a bit frowned on you know. I suppose she caught a bit of trade because a lot of people came at the weekend to go up the Dane Valley.

Peter Whittaker came every Friday night from Macclesfield. He was a greengrocer and he had a horse and a flat cart. He didn't come very early; it'd be 7 or 8 o'clock at night, even in winter. He had a lantern on the front and a bell and he came in the most atrocious weather with an old sack round his shoulders. He never failed to come; he was a poor little old man really, I felt sorry for him, the horse as well. He went right up to Heaton and you'd hear him going back, trotting down the Marsh at 10 or 11 o'clock.

The milk train went at 8 o'clock before it was collected by lorry and it was an eye-opener to see the farmers coming down to it. It used to be like a chariot race down the Marsh, it did really. You'd be amazed at the speed that these horses and floats would go at, to get in time for the train. There used to be quite a procession of them, not galloping, but trotting very, very fast indeed. I can see them now with the churns in the floats and the driver would be standing there, holding the reins tight and sort of leaning backwards. Then half an hour later, they'd come back like a snail, the men reading the papers and letting the horse go on. It was every day of the week, Sunday included.

Mrs Cave and her daughters, Maria, Lizzie and Fanny, lived just past the station. She made oatcakes and Lizzie used to come to our house; perhaps the others went round with them as well. She had a great big market basket with them in, they'd be ever so heavy, all covered up with a white cloth. She came every week. Fanny went round with the post, she always wore clogs.

Uncle Jim Goodfellow had some land up the old road opposite Redway. He didn't farm in a big way at all, but when his hay was ready, everyone had to turn out and help, it had got to be done straightaway. My mother was very good at haymaking, she'd been brought up to it, but my dad wasn't, he was a town man and he never got the knack of it, he hated it, but it had to be got in, all in a big sweat.

Billy Biddulph by Alley Lane.

Father was a great one for walking; he'd go off up the Dane Valley to Ludchurch or Three Shires Head and think nothing of it. I used to walk a lot with friends and at weekends or light nights father gave us shoes, clogs or boots to deliver. We liked doing it, it was somewhere to go. We walked miles, we were only 10 or 11 and we were always instructed by my father that if anyone offered us money, you're not to have any. He wasn't going to have anybody think we did it for money, but I don't remember anyone offering us any.

1928 Wakes Sunday, Mum's relations came to visit.

John Nadin, Fred Earle, William Bowler, Bill Gibson, Harry Twigg.

Ethel Goodfellow

My maternal grandfather was a blacksmith at the bottom of Dial Lane. So mother, Harriet Wood, lived just in Staffordshire and father, William Bowler, came from Weathercock Farm at Timbersbrook, over the border in Cheshire. Soon after they married, they moved up to Lancashire; grandfather had gone up there before them and in the Bowler family, what one did, another soon followed.

After a while, Rushton Hall Farm came up to rent, father applied for it and got it. So in 1918, when I was 3 years old, we moved to there. A train was hired to bring the furniture, the cattle, everything. Soon after that, the 'flu came. There had been a sale at Fenton Farm at the back of the Cloud, and all the Bowlers from round about had been along including father. Well he got it; he and my sister had double pneumonia. Mum and I got it; Granny Wood came to look after us. My sister, Gladys was twelve and she had it least and got up. Then she had a relapse and died. I can just remember them bringing her in the coffin into the bedroom for mum to see. Where the sale was held, they lost two children; it was terrible, Grandma Bowler died with it too.

Rushton Hall was 150 acres and rented from the Antrobus estate, which covered Rushton James and Horton Hay. The estate was up for sale in 1921 and we bought the farm in 1924. It was a mixed farm, corn and green crop bordering Beat Lane and the rest meadow and pasture grass with poultry near home - my mother's domain. We fetched drinking water from down the main road in churns. There was a pump in the yard, but the water was very hard and we didn't like drinking it. Dad put a ram in from the Dingle brook and there was a pond that they let the cows out to in winter. It's gone now, but there were newts, frogs and all sorts in it.

There were up to forty cows, a lot then - we were one of the biggest milk producers in the area. We only made cheese when we had to, if the milk was stopped. One bedroom floor had stains all over it where previously they'd had cheeses stored. Harry Twigg was cowman and Jake Steele the horseman. Jake was always bent double in later life; his feet had been

Rushton Hall 1926. First 'milk lorry'.

badly injured in the first war with trench foot. There'd be extra men to help with haymaking, draining or threshing.

There was a good range of buildings on three sides of the yard. Facing the house was the barn, an open square with lofts on each side. On the right loft was a threshing machine and on the left a chopper with gearing in-between. In the field at the

Dad with Pippin at Biddulph Show, 1920s.

back was a gin ring with three heavy wooden shafts. We often used two horses each attached to a shaft and they walked round and round to provide the power to work the machinery.

I went to Rushton School, where I once had the stick for sliding on the Feeder when it was frozen. We had a hand-bell group, while the boys had a drum and fife band. Mr Banks taught us how to play them. It was Oakapple day on May 29th and you had to wear a sprig of oak or your legs were lashed with nettles by the boys. That was in the 1920s.

There was a custom of fastening a rope across the Oak Bridge or up by the church if there was a wedding and the bride and groom had to pay to cross. I wanted to watch once when one of the teachers was getting married and missed it. I'd run up to Daniels Well to get some water - the water at school was dreadful - I had a tin of Eiffel Tower lemonade powder and you put a spoonful into your water to make lemonade.

We went to the church Sunday school, probably because it was closer. It was held before the service in the morning and again at 2 o'clock. The younger ones sat in the Brocklehurst pew and the older ones went up in the gallery. When I was ten in 1925, I was chosen to be the Well-dressing Queen; I was thrilled. My sister made my dress and on the

With neice, Gladys.

day I got ready at Mrs Turnock's, opposite the school gate. If the Congleton band was playing, they came along on the train and accompanied the Queen, and if she lived near by, she was fetched from home. I remember it drizzled all afternoon. After the ceremony at the well, I was carried back to the schoolyard to a lovely throne which was quite high. There were three

Sir Philip Brocklehurst and his mother Lady Annie.

rows of children, the page boys at the top. They came up to me in twos and bowed and I bowed back. Then we watched the maypole dancing and after that were sports and the produce show. It was a big do.

When I was twelve, I went to Westwood High School until I was sixteen. I walked down to Cliffe Park station to catch the train. You had to wear woolly stockings all year, there was no summer uniform then, and you got very hot, so on the train home, we'd stick our legs out of the window to cool down.

There was a tennis club by Ballast Hole Bridge. It had two courts and a nice hut. The vicar, Rev G. Herbert Smith was chairman and I was often his partner. We had matches with Rudyard and Bosley; they had courts as well. Mr J. Trueman was the linesman and did the mowing; he had a push mower. We had a lovely time; we'd play as often as we could. We closed in autumn 1939 and never started up again because of the war.

Late 1920s. Far left, Alice Dale. Right, Tom Sumner, Phoebe Brassington, Ethel.

At fourteen, I joined others for Confirmation lessons with the vicar at school and three of us joined the choir, Annie Sumner, Olive Dakin and me. There were nine girls altogether in the Swythamley pews and two rows of little boys and two rows of men in the chancel. It was a big choir, quite a picture going down the aisle. Mr and Mrs A Condliffe, the vergers, would light the stove on Saturday and go down again last thing to make it up, and then again early the next morning. They also washed the choir laundry and starched it for special occasions. It was kept in a wardrobe in the vestry.

The Brocklehurst family came to special services. At Easter, the vicar took Holy Communion at 7am and 8am, then Annie, Lady Brocklehurst, sent her chauffeur to fetch him to Swythamley for 9 o'clock, then back to Rushton for 10.30. The Easter collection went to the vicar, on Whit Sunday it was for the choir fund, and a fancy dress dance on Shrove Tuesday paid for the choir trip.

In 1904, the year my husband Jim was born, his parents moved into the house and shop which they had built called Marsh View. The hours were long, opening at eight in the morning for the milk floats on their return journey home from the station, until eight or nine at night. Many goods came in bulk; flour in 7lb calico bags inside a large hessian sack. Lard was in a light galvanised bucket, biscuits loose in big tins and weighed out as required. The bread was not wrapped when delivered, the milk bread came by pony and van from Tattons in Leek, the plain from a bakery in Congleton. Each loaf was wrapped in tissue paper when sold. During the first war the Congleton firm had a large gas bag on top of their petrol van; as the gas emptied it used to flap about in the wind and frighten the animals.

A wooden barrel held the vinegar. Customers brought their own bottle, which was filled from a tap through a tun-dish into the bottle. Boiled sweets were a ha'penny an ounce. Tobacco and cigarettes were kept in a wooden case with a bowed glass front. Several cheeses would be bought from a local farmer and stood on brown paper on a bedroom floor. They had to be turned regularly until ripe for selling. Paraffin was stored in a 50 gallon container in the outside wash house and was pumped up into a measure to fill a customer's container.

'Pig Day' was extra busy . This came round once a month in winter. Jim's father bought three or four pigs from a farmer; they were killed on the farm and the carcasses delivered on the Thursday morning and taken straight down into the cellar. The previous weekend, Jim would have been sent round to call on people to see if they wanted any pork. A local butcher came to cut up the meat to the required orders and Jim's eldest sister took it out to the customers. The sides of bacon were salted on the salting stone in the cellar and the hams were cured in a large wooden vat. There were strong hooks in the cellar ceiling and in the passage to the back door to hang them on to dry. The bacon and ham were sold in the shop and were very popular with visitors who stayed in the village. The fat was rendered down for lard in the kitchen oven and sold in the shop. The pigs' heads were boiled and the meat pressed to make brawn.

Jim's father was also an agent for Lever's Animal feeds and he had a coal depot at Rushton station. When Jim went on his own, he let the coal job go, he was too busy with the corn and sold Dixon, Brown and Tate's seeds. We also decided against keeping the shop open when we married in 1936. Jim was the Macclesfield agent for Lever's Feeds. He had a large round; Adlington and all up around the Wildboarclough area and from Biddulph Moor to Leek. In one of the bad blizzards, people were desperate at Wildboarclough and he took what bread Mrs Turnock could spare with him.

He stood at Leek Cattle Market on a Wednesday, when it was in the middle of town. He did a lot of business from his car, that was his office. When he got home at night, he had to write the orders up and put them out for the lorry driver to pick up the next morning on their way to Birkenhead. Ben Wilde did a lot of our delivering and Ron Allen often drove for him. It was a long job doing the orders on a Wednesday night - we broke at 9.30 for a meal of sausages, then went on until midnight. In wartime and afterwards until 1953, when rationing was on, that made more work; the farmers had to hand Jim their coupons when they ordered the corn and he had to sort them out; everything had to balance.

Before the war, the police came round asking people if they would like to volunteer for the Observer Corps and a group was set up in Rushton. Some proved to be too old or their eyesight wasn't good enough - *"Ah'm neow good fer this!"* Jim had always been interested in aircraft and had very good long sight, so he became one of the main men. They had to train and go to Derby to take tests and then take tests on a regular basis locally. The master test was to identify the front view of planes on a screen and Jim got 84 out of 100. So then he was also a part time instructor, he had classes at the school.

In the N group were 3 posts; Rushton was N3, Hartington N1 and Ipstones N2. Gawsworth were in M group. They had to identify and plot the course of passing planes and report to Derby HQ, *"N3 calling, N3 calling, plane heard,"* and report the description and course. They would be looking out for enemy planes on the way to Manchester or Liverpool. A lot of planes came by Rushton, they used Rudyard Lake for navigation.

The Observer post was on the top of Malkin's bank on the way to Wormhill. In the first winter there was no shelter at all, just the sandbags; then after that the little hut was built, but someone had to be in the circle all the time. There were three full-timers, Jim, Mr Keen, a retired policeman, and Mr Mo Brown. They did 8 hour shifts, 6-2, 2-10 and 10-6. The part-timers did 4 hrs and there was always two on duty, a full-timer and a part-timer.

Jim loved the job, apart from the cold. He lost part of his hearing during a thunderstorm, when lightning struck the wires; they weren't allowed to take their headphones off. He never liked storms afterwards. In summer they were looking up at the sky all the time and he got so suntanned people thought that he was from abroad. The milk in the tea curdled, so he got used to drinking it without.

He always had his supper before he went on the nightshift; then hung his bag up in the hut with a bit of food in. If he felt like a drink or a bite, the other man would take over. One night, he found there'd been a mouse in the bag and made a hole through his sandwich. My little dog, Spotty, always started barking long before I heard planes coming - and just at the German ones. We were always down to our last 6d in those days, so the Observer's pay came in very handy. Jim kept up the corn selling. He was that tired; he nearly crashed his vehicle several times, finding himself on grass verges.

The Observer Corps had the idea of going underground on the road to Wormhill but it wasn't needed, with the war ending. The Corps kept going until quite recently.

Water - The Marsh didn't get its name for nothing; unless the land is well looked after it soon goes back to rushes. Although it may seem as if there is water everywhere and an underground lake, people in the early part of last century were fetching their drinking water in buckets from wells. St Daniel's well up the Old Road to Leek was the most convenient. The water in St Daniels would disappear for months. It was said, *"When Daniels goes dry, it foretells a disaster for the country"*. It did go dry before the war and even after we had

Back:-- Smith, J. Allen, T. Cope, A. Allen, N. Dale, G. Mee, E. Higginbottom, B. Cook, -- Dawson, W. Holland
Front: -- Smith, J. Goodfellow, L. Price, W. Hulme, W. Keen, M. Brown.

Jim and Leslie Price, 1944.

piped water, if I heard it had gone dry, a little spasm of fear would go through me!

When it had gone dry, people started to fetch their water from Meadow Spring, also known as St Anne's well, along Mr Henry Hine's field below the Feeder. This was beautiful water; it came gushing out of the ground. Mr Hine complained about the trespass on his land and it wasn't ideal for people going there - the ground was wet and uneven. By the time you got back to the road, part of the water had been spilt. In 1921, another dry period, a few brave people sowed the seeds about harnessing the water from Meadow Spring which flowed away down the brook to the River Dane. A meeting was called and most householders agreed it was a good idea. Mr Henry Hine didn't know what he wanted and took to his bed! Everyone paid £13 for the work done. A solicitor was consulted and plans drawn up to install a water ram to convey water from the spring to an existing water main belonging to Messrs James Goodfellow snr and Thomas Buxton, situated by the Feeder bridge opposite the Royal Oak. Householders also agreed to install a storage tank and pay a proportionate share of any future maintenance needed. Surplus water was pumped to Daniel's well, so that anyone else could use it.

The ram always seemed to break down in the day time and it fell to Jim or Alf Holland to start it again. I remember Jim coming back from work, putting on his wellingtons and slop and sighing at the thought of going to start it yet again.

It worked well for years until the pipes corroded - I remember when Sunday afternoons were taken up running a trickle of water into buckets for the outside washing boiler ready for Monday wash day. Then we sank a well in the orchard; the water came in when we got down 15 feet. We had an electric pump in the kitchen, but again the water was hard and not nice. Eventually we had a public supply from Rudyard, which is pumped to Franks Bank and runs down by gravity. Meadow Spring water now supplies Congleton.

Years ago, I was picking blackberries in Minnie's field near the ram and it was making its last gasps - it seemed so sad.

Early days in 1939.

James Cotterill at Woodhouse Green.

Ralph Steele.

1927. Mr Needham, Joe and Charlie.

1952. Needham family at Overhouses.

Elsie Needham

I was born and brought up at Thorncliffe. When I left school, I helped at home for a while, then went to work at Bradnop, doing farm work and housework, before getting a job at Rudyard Hall Farm, working for Wains. They had a milk round in Leek and I was a dairymaid there, bottling milk and washing bottles and such like. When Mr and Mrs Charles Dale took the farm on, I stayed with them. They took the milk in a van; it was rare that I went on the round.

It was while I was there that I met Arthur; we met at Christian Endeavour meetings at Gun End chapel. I walked across the fields to Fairboroughs to meet Edith Brough, who went with me. We were married in September 1940. I remember, in the following early summer, a group of soldiers turned up at Overhouses Farm and took the place over for a few days. There'd be about 150 of them. They could just do things like that then with the war being on. We thought they were testing communication equipment, we were quite secluded there. We hadn't got all the house furnished so the officers and their batmen occupied two rooms, one up and one down. They brought cooking equipment and camp beds. The other men slept in the farm buildings. They queued up for their rations. We had to work round them; it was quite an interesting experience.

The 1947 winter was really tough for us. Jim Salt from Primrose used to help us. They had to dig out to get the milk away and get some corn in, then it would blow it all back in again. I was expecting at the time, but luckily the worst was over by 23rd March, when Michael was born. I remember Arthur going to the funeral of Tom Gaskill of Broad Moss. They couldn't get by the roads, so the coffin had to be carried up the hill through the fields. He said what a struggle it was and such a job helping his wife along.

We were always involved with Rushton Chapel; in 1955 Arthur went on the full plan as a local preacher - he completed nearly 40 years before retiring. He was a parish councillor for Heaton. His father, James, was a county councillor. I think when he finished, Charles Dale followed for a while, then Arthur. He did about 20 years, he really enjoyed it; but it meant he was away from home a lot, so I was left to keep things running smoothly.

Elsie.

Charlie and Joe going milking, mid-1920s.

John Lockett

I was born at Ball Haye Green in Leek and when I was about one year old we moved to Rushton Bank Farm. Dad rented the fields by the church, 14 or 15 acres, from Ralph Goldstraw of Wellbeach Farm and his farm buildings as well. When Mr Goldstraw died, dad continued to rent it from his daughter, Miss Goldstraw. Well she didn't like me and I didn't like her. Around every firework time, we'd lay some fireworks and the rest of the year she'd try and get me in deep mire for it. We always managed to keep one jump ahead though. She was a teacher, but luckily never taught me. I may have been the bane of her life.

There were these fireworks called Little Demons and on one memorable occasion, there was Phillip Dale, Reg Trueman and me. Reg, the brains of the outfit, had bound six of these bangers together using airfix wire and connected a fuse to all six. We put it in Miss Goldstraw's lean-to shed at the back under a dustbin lid, lit it and bolted. The explosion that followed could have been heard in Macclesfield. She was gunning for me the next morning, but I denied all knowledge. She asked where I'd been the night before and I said, *"Down at Phil's, weighing his ducks."* When Phillip got on the school bus at The Hanging Gate, she asked him what we'd been doing. *"Oh, down at my house, playing darts."* But we still denied it. She was after me all the time; it was an ongoing battle of wits.

Dad hand-milked 10 or 12 cows and we walked them round to the Church fields afterwards. We also grazed the 'Long Meadow', the road sides on Bandridge Lane. This was in the 1950s; it was rare for any vehicle to come. I was about 8 years old, dad would be at the Crown end with his *Farmers' Weekly*, or if he was fortunate, someone came for a chat. I was at the other end, bored to death, stopping them going back until they'd filled themselves; then eaten with gnats, we'd venture home again.

Frank Condliffe, the verger mowed all the grass in the churchyard with a scythe once a year and dad and I used to go across with forks, gather it up and throw it over the hedge for our cows to eat. There's a tall old Scot's Pine tree as you go through the church gates, near the sundial. There was an old carrion crow nesting in it one year and Mr Condliffe and dad between them decided this bird had to go. We'd got two wooden ladders, so dad carried them across and spliced them together with rope and with great difficulty they reared them up and made me go up to throw the eggs or young birds out. I was petrified, but I'd got to do it, you did as you were told then. I was only little and it was a long way up.

Dad worked full time at Bosley Wood Treatment; he was a joiner there for 40 years. There was about 8 acres of hay to make and apart from the mowing and carting, it was all done by hand, so mum and granddad were left to do most of that. Reg Beswick used to mow it for us.

With cousin Margaret in the hay field.

Around this time the De Trafford vault in the church was opened up for repairs and dry rot treatment. A special licence had to be got to do it. Dad and I and Tom Sumner went along to have a look. The vicar, Mr Corliss and Mr Condliffe were also there. What struck me most was the beautiful silver engraving on the lead coffins and a pile of bones in the corner. I was fascinated.

When we were young, the winters were worse than they are now. When Rushton Bank was covered in snow, all the youngsters from nearby gathered for sledging down the road. My sister, Rosemary; Bernard and Doreen Brown, Fred Robinson and numerous others. We'd sledge back and to 'til all hours of the night. Old Mrs Cooper, who lived in one of the cottages near the bottom of the bank, cleaned her fire out in a morning and threw the ashes onto the road, but by the time we'd sledged for half an hour the following night, we were going that fast by the time you got there, you went straight over. If you were good enough you could get round to the Knot. Fantastic! Dad became an artist at standing two churns of milk on a sledge and going down. He didn't go as fast as us of course; he rode part of the way himself down to the Knot, where the lorry picked them up. Calves too were put in a sack with their heads sticking out and the corners of the bag tied, so they couldn't

Haymaking 1949. Dad, Mary Sunter, Margaret, me, Rosemary and Lassie.

stand up. They were left at the Knot for the Moss and Lovatt cattle wagon to take them to Leek Market. They were put through the little door that leads to the cellar; if you opened it, there could be 5 or 6 calves waiting to be picked up, all from different farms.

Reg Trueman

My great grandparents, Fred and Carrie Trueman, lived at Bottom Lock, Bosley. It was a smallholding and Fred was the lock-keeper; he maintained the locks and kept the sides of the canal tidy. Grandad James (Jim) was born there around 1890; that was where he learned to swim, he fell in so many times. His father said to him, *"I'll make you safe,"* and tied a rope under his arms and knotted it between his shoulder blades and threw him in saying, *"Right, swim!"* He held on t' th' end oth' rope while granddad splashed and paddled about, until he found he could keep himself up. That's how he learned him swim.

They moved to Top Lock, then to Green Meadow. When granddad left school, he went into service as a farm labourer at Dob Ford, North Rode, later meeting and marrying grandma, who was Hannah Holland, post-mistress at Rushton. She lived with Fred and Carrie while granddad went into the army in the first war; I think he was on the Somme.

Dad was born at Green Meadow, then when granddad came home from the war, they moved to The Anthony, where grandma did bed and breakfast and catered for lorry- drivers. Grandad went to work on the railways as a plate-layer, replacing lines and sleepers and maintaining the 'battersides'. He became the ganger. They lived at The Anthony for the rest of their lives.

At Rushton station about 1905.

Dad farm-laboured at Bosley, before joining up in May 1940. He joined the 16-5th Lancers, a cavalry regiment; but before he saw active service, the horses were taken off them and they were given tanks. So he became a tank driver, spending a lot of time in North Africa, then across to the toe of Italy and fighting all the way up there. He never liked to talk much of his experiences, but he told us of when they were fighting for Monte Casino, a monastery on top of a mountain. The Americans had tried to take it and the Germans had thrown them back several times. They were coming down, walking like you see them on the telly - chin straps swinging, mouthful of gum, rifles on their arms. Dad was standing at the side of his tank with his crew. One came past - he never broke stride, *"You don't want go up there Bub, the bastards are shooting at us and using real bullets as well!"*

Once a bullet came through the observation slit, skimmed dad's eyebrow and hit the radio operator in the face, smashing him to pieces. Dad said he just had to shove him out of the way and keep going, but that really got to him.

He was billeted with an Austrian family, who had a daughter, Helga who thought the world of him. She had visions of coming over till she found out there was a missus. Mother used to get airborne if her name was mentioned ever after.

I am named after my great uncle, Reg Holland, the youngest of the Hollands. He was an officer on a destroyer on North Atlantic Convoy duties in the war. They had just been to America and were loaded with fuel and supplies on their way back. Two days out of New York, they were attacked by a German U-boat. The torpedo struck the magazine and an eye witness said the ship was lifted clean out of the water, where it broke in two and the stern and bows went straight down; there were no survivors.

When dad came home, he went to work for Bartram and Holland, lorry driving; they were family. They carried a lot of milk and feed and would meet at the Smithy garage to swap churns or parts of loads. Les and Alf might start arguing and a fight develop. They could end up rolling about in the mud, as it was then down Smithy Lane. Their stepfather, Bill Bartram, would pick them up, one in each hand and smack their heads together, saying, *"Now behave!"* I remember him when he visited the Anthony, a giant of a man - when he sat in the armchair it seemed to spread. His hands were like massive dinner plates. But he was the pleasantest, most jovial man you could see; his eyes used to twinkle.

I spent a lot of time at The Anthony; I went there after school - mother and dad were at work. Mum used to come home on the ten past six train and I would walk home with her. I helped granddad, he'd got pigs and hens and milked his cows by hand. He once had a blue cow and one day at school not long after he'd had her, Mr Banks told us to draw an animal and I drew this blue cow. I was less than 11 yrs old and I thought I'd done a good job, but he ripped a strip off me and gave me the cane for it. He'd never seen such rubbish, a blue cow, no such thing! I told granddad and he did just expound about Harold Banks. *"He wants to get out of that school and take a look around!"*

At school you had to walk on tip-toe, even with clogs on, and work in silence. The boys sat nearest to him and the girls on the other side. One day someone started flicking bits of paper at the girls and they were flicking it back. *"Go and fetch Uncle Peter."* And one of the boys fetched the cane. It was a yard long and there was a ceremony as it was fetched. He stood it in the waste paper basket ready; but we wouldn't be told. Everybody out; girls first, one stroke on each hand. Everybody had a measured dose; his arm went back 'til the cane touched his behind, then as it whistled over, his arm was straight at the top and he'd positioned you with your hand flat out, thumb back for it to strike across the base of your fingers and to hit the floor. The boys had two strokes on each hand.

One fête day, on the school yard, Mr Banks had set up a blackboard and chalked a man on it holding balloons. Then he pinned blown up balloons onto it. It was so much a go to kick a football and try and burst them. The ball was tied onto a piece of rope with the lace. Freddie Rathmill was kicking, he'd just left school. He'd got some kicks left and all the balloons had burst so Mr Banks was pinning more up. He was a portly man - I was standing with me dad, I can see it now. Me dad nudged Freddie, *"Half a crown says you daren't."* Wham! That ball's on its way and hits Harold straight under his behind. He turns round, stares at Freddie and then walks across to him. Well, when that ball had connected the crowd had erupted in laughter but as Harold progressed down the yard it became a titter, then silence. He got to Freddie and fetched him one from down by his knee, full fist up the side of his face. Freddie cartwheels, nobody says a word. Harold goes back to his blackboard, finishes pinning on the balloons, *"Righto Freddie, your turn still."* Wham, balls on its way, everything's forgotten. Dad had crept a few strides away by then, but he came back and paid up his half crown.

My uncle Derek was a bit of a joker. One day with George Oliver and Alf Holland, he was walking under what's known as Peggy's Lantern, where the millstream goes under the railway line. The footbridge was down, so they were wading through the brook, stooped down; Alf first then George, Derek behind. He had a banger and a tin lid, it must have been planned. He lit the banger, put it on the tin lid and floated it after them. Just as it got behind George, Bang! He leapt forward, catapulted into Alf, who nose-dived into the water with George full-length on top of him. Derek was doubled up with laughter and the pair of them threatened what they'd do to him if they ever caught him.

The Hanging Gate.

In the school holidays, when I was 14, I went with dad to deliver a load of gravel into Manchester. He always did the pools and he'd forgot to fill them in. So he said when we got the other side of Macclesfield, *"Dus want drive?"* *"Ah, I'll drive."* It was a nice new Leyland Comet. I set off nice and steady into Stockport, then came to a set of traffic lights on red. There was a copper just the other side staring intently at me. I said, *"Dad; that copper's looking very intently at me."* He pulled his glasses down, looked over and said, *"Bugger him!"* And carried on doing his pools. The lights changed and away we went. And I've been driving lorries for 48 years since.

Swythamley Hall.

Toft Hall.

Wall Hill.

The Crown.

Wolfdale.

Sylvia Wood

I was born at Feeder Cottage; my parents went there in 1934. Mum was Grace Findlow, from Bearda and dad was Jack Allen, from Coppice Side. He was the water bailiff for British Waterways and his job was to regulate the water flow between the River Dane and Rudyard Lake. He had to work all the weirs and sluices. The Feeder was level, so it was possible to let water either way from the river to the lake or vice versa. Just in the stretch between Thompson Bridge and the Dane were three sluices and an overflow, where water could be let back into the river if there was a storm.

It all had to be cleaned out; they scythed it out, scything the weeds off the bottom thoroughly down to the Lake. He did a lot of it himself, but two men came and helped on that job. They wore waders and threw it out onto the bank and it had to be shifted afterwards. He also mowed all the sides; he made hay of the stretch down to Thompson Bridge, it was all scythe work.

Mother took visitors in and did teas; I remember as a little girl helping to serve teas. All the lemonade and produce was left at the Thompson Bridge and punted up or taken on our little pony and cart or father carried some stuff on the handlebars of his bike. And we kept a few cows, pigs and hens.

Me and my brother, Geoff had to come out of our beds and put camp beds up in the living room to sleep on. The visitors took our rooms; I think mum let three rooms out.

Dad sometimes had to go late at night up to Gig Hall to the weirs to see how much water was coming over if it was flooding. He had to walk up the stone wall which separates the canal and the Dane and go up the steps to the top weir. One night, he hadn't come back, we wondered where he was. He'd actually fell in the Dane, he'd put his torch out and coming down the steps stepped off into the river. With it being in full flood, he was lucky he fell into a pool and managed to get himself out. He turned up wet through - my mother was going mad.

We had an idyllic childhood there; we spent hours in the river rooting for bullnogs under the stones. And watching trees going whizzing by when there was a flood. We walked down to Rushton School every day and went to Sunday school.

If you needed a doctor, he walked from Thompson Bridge. Mother scalded her legs once when I was little, something fell off the range and Dr Pepperdine came everyday to dress her legs. His daughter came and played with us while he was attending to her.

There were quite a lot of fish in the Feeder, pike and bream. I remember my uncle coming to fish. You could see them, the water was clear and fast flowing then and we ate them.

In 1949, we moved to Ivy House, down in Rushton. Dad became a postman till he retired. I think his round was about 18 miles a day, all on foot.

Jack Allen.

Sylvia on the
Feeder side. 1940.

Geoff, David,
Sylvia and Janet.

The Feeder Cottage
in the 1940s.

Norman Rogers

I was only five when we moved from Hawksley Farm down here to Ivy Farm, Heaton. I was sent down to Rushton School, where Harold Banks gave me the cane regularly to keep me in order. It was just a mile to walk. I left at fourteen at the summer holidays 1941. My last year was at Leek High, they had just started taking the 11 year olds from Rushton.

In the first part of the war, some evacuees had come from Manchester - the teacher was billeted with Harold Banks - but they drifted back, not many were left after six months. A whole school came up from London en bloc. They did their schooling in the chapel schoolroom.

Some of us were sent up to the school house and instructed in gardening, the older end did woodwork in a shed. I enjoyed it, there was lots of fun. There's what we called Bella Brook in a deep valley at the back of the chapel, with a bridge over it, and some of us lads would sneak up there at dinnertime and have a smoke, we'd be well out of sight, puffing and gasping; Woodbines, anything we could get. I suppose we'd be 11 or 12 then.

Harold Banks' father, William, had been teacher before, then when he retired, Harold came back and took over so that his parents could stay in the schoolhouse. He was a lay reader at Rushton Church and after the service on a Sunday night; he'd go to the Royal Oak with a couple of bottles in a bag to be filled with beer for the old folks.

I remember one day when I was a child, being in the garden and seeing a Hawker biplane flying about. It was not unlike a Hurricane, but with two wings. I think the pilot was a friend of the people at Barleyford and he'd swoop and dive through the yard. Well this day he misjudged it and crashed into the trees over there, I heard the crash. We went down to look some time after.

When I left school, I stopped at home. We kept just over thirty milkers and enough young stock coming along to keep things going. Father used to do a bit of dealing and trading, he'd buy off Fred Robinson and Joe Cantrill. He was late going TT attested, (Tuberculin Tested) and some of the cattle that he'd bought would have been other people's rejects. Some of them had to go. We had always kept a bull but he went on his second test and we never had another; we used the AI after that.

We managed mainly with two horses; that was my job, I enjoyed it. I started with one and a cart and at haytime a tedding machine and a swath turner; then graduated to two horses on the mower. Thomas, the last horse we had, was a topper; you could set him mowing and put him up against the crop and he'd follow along the swathes, you hardly needed to steer him. Same if you were ploughing with him, he was great if he'd got something to follow along. When you got to the headland and turned round he could see automatically where to go; he knew his job. He was never shod and you always had to put his gears, his collar and chains on outside. If you didn't and as he came out through the door his chains or something caught or touched, he'd panic. Same if you were bringing a wide implement through a gate, you had to be very careful - *"Are we going to miss?"* He'd be agitated if anything touched. And on 5th November we had to put him in the far fields out of the way from the village and any fireworks or he'd go berserk.

One day there was a big fog and I was loading turnips up in the top field. And now and then you could just see the shadowy figures of horse's heads over the wall. Well my horse could stand it no longer, he was for off. I just managed to sprint and grab him in time.

Another horse was Dobbin, an Irish horse, quiet and soft as a mop, but I didn't think as much of him, you had to steer him all the time. If you were scuffling green crop like turnips or soiling potatoes up, Thomas kept between the rows while Dobbin would be slopping his feet about and perhaps damaging the crop.

I sometimes worked two horses in tandem with chains, same as for muck carting up top. Some people used horses in tandem for carting hay with a hayloader behind the cart.

In 1947 we had to cart the milk down to Rushton for quite a few weeks. The lane was ridded and Jack Heathcote from Heaton Hall had a little cart and we used Thomas, who because he wasn't shod, the snow didn't stick in his shoes and ball up under his feet. All the milk out of Heaton went on that little cart down to Bartram Holland's.

Our last horse went in 1953 or 54, it was a sad occasion to see them go, you could talk to them while you were working. But now we could use the ground that had kept them to keep extra young stock. We couldn't keep more milkers without making more accommodation, so we didn't need to buy in stock.

A lot of horses were commandeered in the first war; if you'd got two horses, they wanted one. You might have a two-horse mowing machine, but they'd say, *"You must share a horse with your neighbour"*. Thousands were killed.

Uncle Ernest had a horse inclined to run away. At Axstones Springs in the old meadow, he was helping Uncle George cart some hay and they were building a stack. Uncle Ernest was on the stack, Uncle George on the cart. They'd just finished unloading when the top of the stack slipped off and Uncle Ernest with it. The horse took off across the steep bank side, Uncle George jumped out before it got to the steepest part, when the cart turned over. Uncle Ernest came up through this yard as white as a sheet.

I remember a character called Billy Mountford who lodged at Heaton Lowe. He was a roadman and he liked his drink. Mrs Fernihough was remonstrating with him one day, *"Bill, if you carry on drinking like this, there won't be enough money to bury you."* His reply was, *"Bertha, when didst ever hear of 'em leavin' anybody on th' top"*. And when he was in the army they were yelling at him, *"We tame lions here!"* He said, *"We eat the buggers where I come from!"* He'd always got an answer.

Arthur Needham
going ploughing
with Fanny and
Captain, 1938.

Two-horse mower
at Rudyard.

Ralph Steele
at Heaton
House.

Ernest Rogers

Our dad, James Rogers was born at Old Hay Top. He never went to school 'til he was seven, when Gun End School was first opened in 1902. He left at thirteen. Grandad Rogers rented the farm from the Swythamley Estate, the same as our other grandad, Charles Moss, who rented New House Farm, at Meerbrook. He was the youngest tenant at one time.

Uncle Ernest was three years and three months younger than dad and when he left school, dad went working for John Turnock at Wormhill for twelve months, then for Charles Moss at New House. When the war started they had left New House and moved to Hawksley, near to Gun End.

Dad should have gone in the first war, but Charles Moss was then running two farms; he'd taken Hawksley, and he owned Horse Haylands at Meerbrook and dad was needed on the farms. We used to have a khaki armband with a red crown on, which was father's, to show he was in a reserved occupation. Uncle Ernest should have gone too, but he'd had an accident, when a horse had kicked a stone up and hit him in the eye and left him partially sighted.

They used to fetch all sorts of stuff from Rushton Station to Old Hay Top; coal, lime, wet beet pulp. Uncle Ernest and grandfather Rogers were going down Rushton Marsh to the station one day to fetch something with a young horse they were breaking in. One of them walked on each side. Someone let a gun off and the horse took fright. Ernest pulled it to him to get it off his father and it knocked him down and trampled him. The marks of the hooves were on his back. Mr James Goodfellow was one of the first to have a car and he took him to the doctor's. He was never able to pitch hay that summer.

In 1920 dad went to work for Joe Goodfellow at Hugbridge for six years. He said it was the easiest years he had in his life and the best wage.

Around 1921, grandad Moss bought Hawksley from the Swythamley Estate. He paid about £2,000 for it, just over eighty acres. He later sold it after buying Ivy Farm, here and keeping twenty-four acres to go with it. He had mortgages round his neck all his life; he was married

With Mary Allen at Hawksley.

young and had a hard life of it. When Rock House next door came empty, he bought that because it's mixed up in this; but he hadn't the money and had to have a mortgage; when he died our father had to pay it off.

At Hawksley, they took the milk down to Rushton Station. In 1926, when the railways went on strike, the young fellows from Rushton; Bill Bartram and Sam Moss got bits of trucks and went round farms picking the milk up. Mother said Bill Bartram started by taking the back seats out of an old taxi and taking milk to Manchester; dad was one of his first customers.

In Heaton, there was the Black Horse pub, owned by Mr Tompkinson of Heaton House. Old Sir Philip and him were enemies and Sir Philip was responsible for getting the license taken and closing the pub down. He said it was a meeting place for poachers. This was around the time of the first war.

Next door to us is Well Cottage and next to that is Dolly's Well. It never goes dry. Along with the well on Heaton Bank, near the Pinfold, it would be where the village fetched their water from.

> Lurphamley
> Nov 20th. 1871.
>
> Dear Sir,
>
> 5 Poachers will be up on Wednesday 3 of them have been convicted before, they were a gang of 8, we saw 3 others, who escaped — we thought they meant a rescue, and as I thought also some of the 5 had given wrong names I sent them in a conveyance for the police to examine them — They gave me up 3 dogs, nets, rabbits and a ferret, 1 dog has since escaped — I claim as L? of the Manor all the spoil — On Nov 12 1863 before J Sneyd Esqr. & J Russell James & Wm Cooker were convicted for Night Poaching, I kept their dog and was sued in the County Court for it before Sir Walter Riddell he gave the Verdict in my favour — Please look up this case —
>
> Yours truly
> P. L. Brocklehurst

We had a tail pump in our kitchen, pulling from a glazed brick tank which caught the overflow from Dolly's Well. In 1946, we had an engine and pump to fill our tanks; we didn't waste any water then. All the farms round here on these dry sandy banks were short of water; Coppice Side, Heaton House, Intakes. At one time they tried windmills to raise water, but sand got in the works when the water table dropped and they had to take the pipes up. Dale's at Intakes had a go at digging a well; a cow got in it once. And there was a well at Heaton House which old man Steele fell in and injured himself. After the first war, they had a go at putting a hydraulic ram in near Axstones, to take water up to Heaton House. Ralph Steele told me one of his brother George's first jobs after coming home from the war was digging a trench from the back of the Burrows for the pipe to the ram and what a tough job it was.

We had a David Brown Cropmaster, when the horses went. We thought it was wonderful except the only means of starting it was the starting handle. We kept it under this zinc-roofed shed outside and it was difficult to start on a frosty morning. One of us swung the handle a bit, then the other. There was a Salop trailer came with it, with sideboards and gates for haymaking. It's only lately been sawn up for firewood.

We changed it for a David Brown 30D, second-hand from down in Cheshire. It was a bit rough, with one tyre worn flat. So it was resprayed and the wheels swapped off the old Cropmaster. There was a battery on either side for starting; it made life easier.

We had a little lift-up shed as grandfather had had put up. There was a girder on each corner with brackets and pegs; and a handle like a railway signal to raise the roof or let it down. It was alright for loose hay, but not so good for bales. We had a Welger baler; it made batten bales, a bit like a sheaf, not compressed much; but we couldn't get all the hay inside with that. It wasn't much better than carting loose hay. So we didn't keep that long; we did a deal with Blakemore and Chell and had a Jones baler, a topper!

I did a fair bit of hand milking, but Norman did it mainly when we had the buckets; we used cans till we finished in 1994, tipping them into the bulk tank. Norman did the tractor work too. I had the barrow and shovel. Jim Dowley, the postman said to me, *"If ever yo 'ave a coat of arms, yo mun 'ave a brush on it, you're always sweepin' the yard."*

We kept quite a few hens and a flock of thirty odd ducks. We had 12 by 8 foot Pilkington hencotes, some on runners with towing hooks on the end. In summertime we took the hencotes, hens and all, over th' other side o' th' farm onto fresh ground. We loaded the horse and cart up with a wooden barrel or two of corn and churns of water to take to them. Light nights, Norman could be very late shutting them in; eleven o'clock or after.

We took the eggs in the car, a 1937 Morris 10. It hadn't a proper boot; we lifted the back seat up and put groceries in there, and had a carrier on the back and put some egg boxes on that, and so many more inside. Then we took them to Torr's, at Ryles Park, Macclesfield; they were milk retailers.

I've always been a chapel man; mum was church, her father was a sidesman at Rushton. Our grandfather, James Rogers was chapel steward and Sunday school teacher at Gun End. Norman's like dad; he hadn't much time for it, and called them *"Dog collar men."*

Jack Heathcote, Eric Heath, Frank Heathcote, 1957.

1911/1912

1911/1912. Teacher Florence Cotterill, later Mrs Goodfellow.

May Queen 1911/1912.
The old pound or pinfold can be seen on the wall of the Royal Oak, on the left of this photo.

Back row: Minnie Buckley, Victor
Buckley, -- --, Hilda Buckley
Front: -- --, James Davenport, Lily
Davenport, Lydia Hine, -- --, -- --

Below:
Mrs Mary Goodfellow,
Mrs Cantrill, Mrs Bowler,
Mrs Ethel Goodfellow.

Mr Tom Massey, centre,
Albert Meakin, right.

Ralph Steele on the right.

David Goodfellow 1955.

Below: Ralph Steele Snr in the 1930s

Arthur and
Doris Needham

Christine Chester

My mother's family came to Wolfdale; John Howarth bought it in1818. In the 1840-1860s, Rev James Bostock, vicar of Wincle, lived there and only moved to Wincle when they built the vicarage. Great, great grandfather, George Bostock came next, then his daughter, Sarah Mariah and her son Fred, my grandfather. My mother was very fond of Wolfdale and persuaded father to buy it when grandfather died.

I can just remember bells in the kitchen, so you could summon the servants. There were two big cooking ranges, one in the kitchen and one in the scullery kitchen; and an oatcake baker with a shiny top and a little fire in it. Pikelets and oatcakes were made on it. There was a copper and a milk cooler in the scullery kitchen and until the Milk Marketing Board came in 1933, we could be told at any time, *"No milk till Monday"*. They would have to take the milk down into the cellar and put it into pancheons, skim it and make butter in the end-over-end churn. There was also a big stone cheese press, with a block of stone as big as a table. The winding gear for the press was in the room above, and the press sat on a lead tray so the whey dripped out into it.

In great, great grandfather's time, in1866, there was an outbreak of Rinderpest or cattle plague and I've got a document where he had to apply to the magistrate for permission for the cattle to cross the road to graze the fields below. And in 1923 there was foot and mouth in the young stock at Old Hill, then called Wolfdale Hay, next door. And by the time they came to kill them, they were better and quite frisky. Grandmother said it was a shame to kill them. I have a bill for the fire; railway sleepers and coal, two men to stay awake during the night to tend the fire - and beer, so much strong ale and so much mild ale.

I went to school in the late 1930s and 1940s, to the kindergarten at Leek High school, at that time a wooden building at the Nicholson Institute. Then afterwards to Westwood High School for Girls. I had to run down the fields, rain or shine to Cliffe Park station to

Cliffe Park Station.

CATTLE PLAGUE.

Removal of Animals from one part of a Farm to another part of the same Farm.

We *John Cruso Esq* and *Thomas Carr Esq* two Justices of the Peace acting in and for the County of Stafford, having satisfied ourselves that the Cattle on the Farm belonging to Mr. *George Bostock* of *Rushton* in the said County, Farmer, are free from disease, and that no Cattle Plague exists in the neighbourhood of his Farm, do hereby License the said *George Bostock* to remove the undermentioned Animals to and from one part of his Farm to any other part thereof, until this License shall be revoked by me or by another Justice of the Peace of the said County, *this certificate is given for the Cattle to go to watering across the road —*

DESCRIPTION OF ANIMALS.

No.		No.	
Fifteen	COWS.		BULLOCKS.
	HEIFERS.		OXEN.
	BULLS.		CALVES.

Dated the *13th* day of *Jany* 1866.

John Cruso.

Thomas Carr

Expences of burning cattle with Foot & Mouth Disease

	£	s	d
coal	5	8	0
Fire wood	2	9	6
10 hrs @ 1/6		15	0
" " "		15	0
26 hrs " "	1	19	0
" " "	1	19	0
48 hrs @ 1/-	2	8	0
4 galls oil @ 1/4		5	4
2 galls beer		8	0
2 qts bitter beer		2	2
£	16	9	0

(1981.)

ORDER OF THE MINISTER OF AGRICULTURE AND FISHERIES.

(DATED 12TH DECEMBER, 1923.)

FOOT-AND-MOUTH DISEASE: INFECTED PLACE.

The Minister of Agriculture and Fisheries, by virtue and in exercise of the powers vested in him under the Diseases of Animals Acts, 1894 to 1922, and of every other power enabling him in this behalf, hereby orders as follows :—

The premises mentioned in the Schedule hereto are hereby declared to be a place infected with Foot-and-Mouth Disease.

In witness whereof the Official Seal of the Minister of Agriculture and Fisheries is hereunto affixed this twelfth day of December, nineteen hundred and twenty-three.

L.S.

J. Jackson,
Authorised by the Minister.

SCHEDULE.

Description and Limits of Infected Place.

The shippons and pastures of the Small Holding of Wolfdale Hay, in the occupation of Fred Yates, Wolfdale Farm, in the parish of Rushton James, in the administrative county of Stafford.

(45490d) 150 12/23 H. St

Printed by HIS MAJESTY'S STATIONERY OFFICE PRESS,
11-17, Hare Street, E.2.

catch the train at 12 minutes past 8. I leaned out of the window at Rudyard station to get a ticket, 4d from Mr Cope, the stationmaster, who had a waxed moustache. Bill Smart was a porter. Then through the tunnel to Leek station. There was a bookstall and when it was fish day, Jim Hall the fishmonger had a little flat dray that he pulled with a hinney and he used to meet the train and take the fish up to his shop in Leek.

I walked up into town and school with my aunt, who worked for Sir T and A Wardle. She'd see me into school on Stockwell Street, and then walk down Mill Street to work. At night, mother fetched me home in the car, because there wasn't a suitable train.

The big boys served dinner at school, carrying three or four plates at a time; I must have been a 'bolshie' child and once got cascaded with stewed apple and custard. I spent the afternoon in the headmistress's study in my vest and knickers awaiting collection by mother. I refused school dinners after that and went to Tatton's café with my aunt. When I was nine, I went up to Westwood and war started.

At Wolfdale, they weren't well off for water; they had to turn the cattle out twice a day to drink and there was a well under the house. So when father wanted a better supply for the milkers, he got in Toppy Brown and Mr Moss to dig another well. They had a windlass, like half a mangle, with chains on and either a seat or a bucket on the end. The seat was to lower the man down and the bucket to send the spoil up. And as they dug it they lined it with bricks on edge. First thing every day they sent a candle down on the seat to see if the air was safe. It was at the same time as the tragedy at Woodhouse Green when three men were lost in a well - they had left it for a while, and when they went down again, each in turn was lost, Mr Jackson, his son and young James Cotterill. It would be the black damp. So when these men had disappeared, the police were called, who then fetched the two men working at Wolfdale. Mr Moss went down with breathing apparatus and what he saw distressed him so much he was sick in it and had to be brought up. Rushton was devastated with the shock of it. I was not quite seven but I remember it vividly.

In the same way I remember the plane crash. It was Whit Saturday, 1944. A Stirling bomber was returning on a practice flight to photograph the Menai Bridge by moonlight. They decided to practice cutting one of the engines out and restarting it, but made the mistake of cutting the other engine out on the same side. It wasn't possible to regain control and it crashed into the hillside on the Rudyard side of Cliffe Park. Four survived out of a crew of eight - they bailed out. One landed at Birch Trees and went to Barnslea; one below Cheetham's Garage in a holly bush; one in the mud at the top end of the lake, and one amongst some cows up at the back of Wolfdale. He said afterwards that he was terrified; he'd come down safely by parachute and now was going to be killed by a bull! Dolly Gibson rescued the man in the lake. He was blowing a whistle and shouting for help. She was very brave because it was 2-3am and she wouldn't know what to expect.

On the west bank of the lake, below Cliffe Park, where it's shallow, the Americans had a camp. It was spring 1944 and they were practising driving lorries into about three feet of water, ready for D-day. They made a bridge out into the water and laid metal tracking in sections hinged together on the bed of the lake and drove the lorries in. The exhausts and air intakes were turned up. It was a tented camp; the staff stayed there while lorries came every day, practising and changing. They made a lot of ruts in the track. We used to cycle

Fred Earle at Wolfdale.

round there on a Sunday night to a friend's house, past the Lady of the Lake, mother, father and me regularly for social and supper. We'd play cards and cycle home, while petrol was rationed. Going past the camp, we were stopped by a sentry with a rifle - *"Halt! Who goes there?"*

There was a strong presence of Americans in Leek. Grandfather Sigley took parties of them out with a horse and landau to local village pubs. I can remember the horse, a big Hackney called Billy. I can almost hear him now coming up from Rushton village, stepping out, bang, bang, bang, bang, as he trotted up the road. He was stable kept and very fit.

And once I can remember going to Bakewell and after going up Crowdicote, where it levels out, there were stacks of bombs by the side of the road. I can also remember the ammunition dump going up at Fauld. It even shook the windows at Wolfdale. Our cousin's wife lived nearby and had to take charge of two children who had lost everything, the farm had just vanished, parents, grandparents, livestock, everything. It was the world's largest non-nuclear explosion.

I was very lucky having ponies to ride, and that we'd spare ground to keep them. There was Curly, 14.2, that mother rode, and a solicitor friend of father asked us to take in one of his horses, a thoroughbred mare. The army had had some of his others and he didn't like the way they were kept. She had done point to point racing, she was lovely, you could do anything with her until she got on grass with other horses, then she went. Sadly, a friend brought three more and one kicked her and broke her leg. Father rang Mr Shenton, the knacker, it was Saturday afternoon. He said, *"Would it wait till morning?"* Father nearly burnt the phone wires out. I'll bet she was sold as best beef. Someone's donkey at Pool End got killed and that was sold as mutton.

I rode the district, sometimes with mother, sometimes with friends, sometimes on my own. We had permission from Sir Philip to ride over the roads and tracks on the Swythamley Estate. Sometimes to Ludchurch or Turner's Pool. One of the funniest things was, I was coming back from a ride and there were some old people having a picnic at Eleven Lane Ends. I stopped to say hello, and they must have had a pickle factory, because the man insisted on giving me a 7lb jar of pickled onions; and if you've ever tried to manage a 7lb jar of pickled onions on a fairly lively pony, it's not an easy thing. I got it back safe but I couldn't get off, I had to yell for help.

I feel privileged to have had such a lovely childhood. The roads were relatively traffic free and the local people were good, kind and friendly. I took the horses or ponies to be shod at Pool End Smithy. It was about three miles. I'd try to get there first on a Saturday morning and George's mother would invite me in for a cup of Camp coffee and a biscuit. It was very nice of her. If I wasn't first and George had another horse in which was being a bit difficult, she would pop out and say, *"Now then our George, you'll get killed."* And he would reply, *"Bugger off in the house!"* He had an old Tam hat hanging above the fire in the smoke. I asked him what it was and he said, *"It's my Bug hat, for shoeing lousy horses in."* It was a different world then.

When I first started going, it was 8 shillings to shoe a pony, 15s for a riding horse and 21s (guinea) for a cart horse. There was a notice up of the charges; Blacksmith's suggested price list, and the last line was, Unruly horses according to time. There were stallion cards pinned up. You'd see the Shire stallions out being walked; I loved to see them with their groom, mane and tail done up in ribbons, bridle and surcingle on.

I didn't like the horse sales because a lot would be going for killing - tractors were coming in then. Father had one at the beginning of the war, a converted Dodge lorry. It could do 40 mph. I can remember taking timber, trees that father had cut down, to Corbishley's sawmill to have them planked, sitting on the petrol tank with a four-wheel trailer snaking behind. Then there was an orange Standard Fordson and a green one with spade lugs that Freddie called Sybil, I don't know why. Then one of the first Fordson Majors. Father did contracting, ploughing and corn cutting for people when it became compulsory. He milked about thirty cows, which then would keep two families. Going back to grandfather, he milked thirteen or fourteen; grandmother hand milked 'til she was sixty. And when his mother was unwell, they could afford a nurse.

Grandfather was a horse dealer as well, and when he had a good Hackney type trotter, he sold it into Manchester to the Manchester Evening News. They wanted fast horses to deliver the papers from the printers out to the shops. It was a source of irritation to my grandmother because once they'd got a horse broken, steady and sensible, it went and another youngster took its place.

There was a man at Packsaddle, Mr Godfrey, who bred alsatians for Airforce guard dogs. I was fascinated because he kept goats for milk for the puppies and he had two little Alfa Laval milking machines with dinky little buckets and two teat cups. He had a firearm permit and carried a pistol with him in case any of the dogs turned on him.

Lucy Knight lived in Heaton and kept goats, eight or nine of them. She was a sweet, gentle person and took them browsing round the roadsides. They all came if she called and if a car came and she told them to get in the side, they did. Someone gave me a little white kid, which I bottle-reared. But it had a bad habit; if anyone came on the yard with a car, she'd bounce onto the bonnet, then onto the roof. She had sharp hooves and people didn't like it; so I was told she'd have to go; so she went to Lucy's.

I remember three bad winters back then, 1940, '42 and of course '47, when there were so few resources after the war to deal with it. The Americans were still about and helped keep the main roads open, but cousins up at Hayes Farm, up Coal Pit Lane were marooned for six weeks. Power stations were at full stretch and could hardly keep up. There was a Royal visit planned to South Africa and Sir T and A Wardle had the job of printing some fabrics for the Queen and princesses. They needed some help to turn the machinery, so along went Gordon Rogers of Rudyard with a Standard Fordson tractor and pulley to help. But the strain of working the machinery wrecked the tractor.

In 1940, I lost my two front teeth near the lake overflow, playing ice-hockey before I was safe on skates. And in 1942, I rode my pony from one end of the lake to the other. It had frozen ripply and rough; I stayed close to the bank though. Any boats left out were crushed by the ice.

In winter, my parents and friends went duck shooting on the lake. When meat was rationed anything extra like that or rabbits came in very useful. I didn't like it though because of finding the shot with your teeth. They used the fishermen's punt; the two labradors would climb in. It seemed unsinkable and wouldn't even rock, but it was like

Hanging Gate Corner

trying to row the Queen Mary. The fishing was let to 'Ye Olde Central Angling Society'.

There was a youth hostel at Cliffe Park. I remember lots of people went down our fields to it, walking or cycling. They bought potatoes off us, and had a Guy Fawkes bonfire which was popular. It closed in 1970.

Cattle at Old Hill.

A few more memories:

I was told about Miss Gibson, from the Hanging Gate, taking ducks in a big basket to Leek market. It was before Cliffe Park station was opened in 1905. The ducks escaped and she tried to catch them, tripped and fell and a train ran over her arms. For the rest of her life she had various tools screwed onto her stumps for different jobs.

At Westwood School, there was a Czech refugee who lived at Rudyard, Vera Lowitz. She'd be twelve and one day in the scripture lesson she put her hand up and asked the teacher, *"Pleeze, vot iss immaculate conception?"* The question was met with deadly silence.

And I especially remember Mrs Turnock's lovely homemade bread and lemon-cheese tarts with stars of butter cream!

Tom Sumner

Cutting oats at High Ash:
The oats were cut with a reaper, which was a mowing machine with a platform. There was a man riding on it on a seat and when it was full, he pushed the cut corn off into a heap. All around the field, men were spaced and they tied the sheaves with bunt, which was pieces of straw with two heads of corn twisted one over the other.

After being stooked in the field for a period, it was stacked in round stacks. High Ash had its own stationary threshing machine with a stationary engine on the loft, driven by a Petter Junior petrol engine,

Frances Sumner at High Ash.

which started on petrol, then ran on paraffin. It also chopped chop and pulped turnips. They used chop (hay and straw) mixed with turnips and corn for horse feed.

Rushton mill ground the oats at the Dyehouse mill then. The other mill had closed. Oats were fed to cattle, horses had bran. Gilbert Chapell on the photo had his clogs double tipped to save money. There was beer in the stone jar from a barrel in the cellar; and lemonade in the bottle.

Tom Sumner, Tom Cope, George Sumner, - -, Gilbert Chappell, William Mountford, Tom Heath, John Sumner.

One of the Holland brothers.

Left: Eva Bailey, May Queen.

Well Dressing 1910.

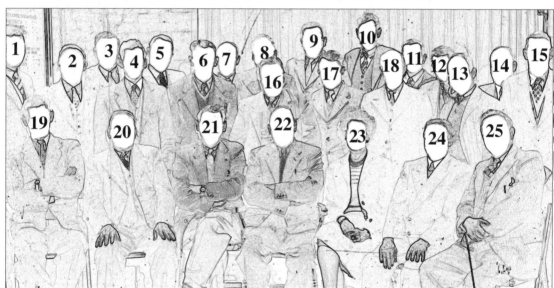

Rushton NFU 1960. Jack Woolley, chairman.

1. Norman Bebington, 2 John Heathcote, 3 Vic Brown, 4 Reg Brown, 5 Herbert Harrison, 6 Mr Johnson (Tithe Barn), 7 Frank Goodfellow, 8 Tom Coates (Ravensclough), 9 -- --. 10 ? Eric Bailey, 11 Bill Oliver, 12 Arthur Eardley, 13 Bob Tideswell, 14 Henry Beardmore, 15 Charlie Needham, 16 John Lockitt, 17 George Wood, 18 Mr Rogers (Heaton), 19 Arthur Needham, 20 Joe Brough, 21 ? Mr Clarke (secretary), 22 Jack Woolley, 23 ? Mrs Clark, 24 Billy Pickford, 25 Ralph Steele.

1950s. Lever's trip to Port Sunlight.

John Woolley

My father, Jack Woolley was a Ministry-licensed egg buyer for North Staffordshire Egg Producers of Chesterton. He also sold eggs into Bramhall, Cheadle Hulme and Wilmslow; going there on a Thursday, Friday and sometimes Saturday. In fact, he never missed going to Cheadle Hulme on a Friday for sixty-two years. He sold to regular customers, door to door. Then on Monday and Tuesday, he travelled the area buying eggs from farms. He'd perhaps go round Rushton, Swythamley, Meerbrook and even as far as Butterton, while mother collected round Biddulph Moor, Lask Edge and Rudyard. Then on Wednesday, they'd go to Leek and stand at the Cock Inn and people brought eggs to him. Later they had a stall in the Buttermarket and bought and sold eggs.

Dad.

They had two vans and at one time a little Bedford 30 cwt lorry with a canvas top. The eggs were moved in 30 dozen boxes; there were six trays of two and a half dozen on each side. On a Sunday morning, he went to three brothers at Alton Towers - Clowes's - and picked up a full load of eggs there.

The egg round business was actually started by his father in law, grandad Mayer, and dad bought it off him in 1932 when he got married. He built it up to 800 customers at its height. Sometimes Margaret went with him in bad weather to open farm gates. One dark night in winter in the Roches area, she was opening a gate, when something ran right past and startled her. In the van lights, they could see it was a wallaby.

At Christmas, he supplied chickens and turkeys, three to four hundred, which he bought in the feather and we all had to help pluck and dress them. In the last few years, he bought them ready-dressed. Young John went with him to help latterly as well, he was determined to complete 60 years in the business.

He sometimes took a load of old hens into Manchester to Sammy Saffir's. In the war, he was once taking a load of blackmarket eggs into Manchester and he broke down. So he asked a policeman to guard the van till he got back to it. It was a good job he never looked inside or dad would have got done.

He started farming on his own as a tenant farmer on a smallholding of six acres, for which he paid £26 rent. He moved to Park Head, Biddulph Park in 1940, then in 1945 purchased Wragg Hall Farm, lock, stock and barrel. He later sold the cows and bought 20 Ayrshires from Kilmarnock, which were the start of the pedigree Earlsway herd. Margaret and I did most of the farming at Wragg Hall, while dad did his eggs.

Start of Ayrshire herd at Wragg Hall.

Earlsway before demolition.

Jesse Perkin.

The farm was used for ten years as an ICI demonstration farm; we did grassland trials. This led to us going to Earlsway farm. Old Jesse Perkin had been left the farm along with someone else, but as he got older, he couldn't cope and for two years up to 1955 it hadn't been farmed at all; the fields were overgrown, the ditches and drains blocked, all gone to rack and ruin. So he was inspected by the War Ag and found wanting - he was the last person to be dispossessed for bad husbandry. The local policeman, Bill Fowler had to handcuff him and lead him into the middle of the road, tears running down his face. Because of the work we'd been doing with ICI, the Ministry of Agriculture asked us to farm it. We let Jesse go back into the house on the understanding that he looked after the stock and buildings.

When the Ministry went to look at the house to take an inventory, they found that he'd never been upstairs for 17 years, all the wallpaper was hanging off and rats and mice had chewed all the bedding up.

In 1958 we got a tenancy between us and Jesse Perkin; 55 acres for £100 rent. He had no money coming in apart from that and little over £1 pension. He always bought a pound and a half of homemade toffee back from Leek on a Wednesday, and he went to the Fox regularly, always sitting in the '£1' seat. At home he stayed in a chair in the living room and never took the ashes from the fire out, just tipped them into a pile in the room. He wore big wellies which he never took off. It caused him to have dreadful ulcers which probably killed him - they turned gangrenous.

He died aged seventy-three; then the co-owner tried to shift us off, but we'd paid off Jesse's mortgage in 1957 and eventually in 1965, we purchased the farm for £6,000. We later knocked the house down and Arthur Bailey built us a new one.

Bibby's trip to Liverpool late 1950s.

Swythamley church.

Sir Philip Brocklehurst, with his pet monkey.

Haymaking early 1960s.

John Woolley Jnr

My great uncle Ernest told me this story. He was the brother of Jack Bowyer of Toft Hall and my grandma Heath. When Jack married Doris Bailey on 21st April 1931, they were married in Swythamley church and Sir Philip's mother, Annie, Lady Brocklehurst played the organ for the service. The reception was in the Tenants Hall and was attended by a lot of people. After a lovely meal, everybody went for a walk around the gardens at Swythamley Hall, with it being nice weather. Uncle Ernest was still eating a ham sandwich and Sir Philip's pet monkey came begging off him. So he gave it a bit, forgetting that it had got mustard on. The monkey spit it out and ran Uncle Ernest all round the garden; he had to run into a rhododendron bush to hide till the monkey had calmed down.

Also during the reception, they ran out of beer, so Michael, Sir Philip's chauffeur went down to the Royal Oak in the Bentley Sports and took uncle Ernest, aged 16, with him for a ride, and let him steer it on the way back. He also said what beautiful stone kennels there were at the hall. Sir Philip bred Staffordshire Bull terriers.

Below Earlsway is Ridding side, where Tom and Lil Mellor lived. Tommy helped us, and we helped him back, but he didn't want any tractors on his land, so all the work had to be done by hand. All the hay was made and carried loose. At that time he never went

Lil Mellor.

Tom Mellor.

to bed, but slept under the hedge for two or three weeks. He could be raking the backswath out and Lil would come with a basket of sandwiches and drink for him and he wouldn't stop till he'd gone all round the field with her following.

When the hay looked ready, Lil got a little nest of hay in her pinafore and took it under

Shearing at Heaton House.

Shearing at Fairboroughs Farm.

Mr Bailey at Toft Hall.

the hedge and tried to light it. If it wouldn't light she wouldn't let us carry it. They carried it on 'stangs' at one time, two poles under a ruck of hay and lift it. Later on, he let us bale and carry one of the fields. And when we rented it after, if we wanted to put a bit of bag muck on, we did it when he'd gone to Leek on a Wednesday, so he didn't see a tractor on it.

He chewed twist, 7ozs a week. He went in hospital once for appendicitis and they couldn't understand why he was full of black juice. But it didn't seem to do him any harm; he was eighty-two when he died.

They milked ten to fifteen cows, all by hand; latterly he milked with one hand, finishing in the 1970s when churns finished. And they kept hens; some laid on the sofa. And they carried their water, there was no mains. But they'd got hearts of gold and always gave me and Liz a 10s note and an orange for Christmas.

At Toft Hall Jan 31st 1926. Doris Bowyer, her mother and her grandmother.

Margaret Woolley

I've always liked poultry from when I was a girl; I once caught diphtheria from a pullet when I was thirteen. It had got fowl typhoid and I'd been carrying it up and down; I was in hospital for six weeks. Mum used to have about 100 day old chicks delivered; they came on the train to Congleton in round boxes. When they arrived, she put newspaper down in front of the fire with chick crumbs on and got a saucer of water and picked each one up to give them a drink and check them over before they went out in the shed to the brooders. I always wanted dad to do breeding but he wouldn't.

So in 1960 at Wragg Hall, I thought I'll start keeping my own poultry. Dad bought me a 12 x 8 foot hencote to start me off. It cost £60, a lot of money then. Then we had another bigger one, 68 x 20 and started putting the numbers up, using lofts as well. I made hot wet mash up for them with cod liver oil. It was a lot of carrying buckets and up steps.

One day grandad John was showing a BOCM man, Mr Almond, round the buildings and he said, *"The standard of management seems very high in the poultry department; are you interested in doing something different?"* And he sent out Mr Andrews, the field officer for Sterling's at Prestbury. When he came, he said he wished I'd been with them before. I had to pass a test and go on probation for a year to see if I could keep up to standard. The hens were Red Links and Silver Links. The eggs went to the hatchery. When they came as chicks, at one time I reared them outside in arks and they had to be individually blood tested for various diseases by the Ministry. At Wragg Hall, I kept a thousand breeding poultry including cocks, which were one to every ten hens. They were put in deep litter after being reared outside.

When we came here to Earlsway, we had the new shed put up, 165 x 45 foot with eight separate pens in and changed policy to all in, all out. They came in at eighteen weeks. We later changed from breeding egg layers to broilers, dealing with J.P. Woods of Craven Arms. Then the parent stock went out at sixty weeks, the hens weighing 13lbs and the cocks 15lbs. They kept very well because they were rationed. We rarely had health problems because I

could tell when something was going to happen and nipped it in the bud. I always checked them last thing at night, listening for little noises like a cough which could be the start of infectious bronchitis. As I walked through them, they made a contented noise almost like a cat's purr; I could step over them as they dust-bathed, they never moved.

We owned the hybrids, but not the broilers, they were on contract. We were paid £5 for every hundred saleable chicks when we finished in December 2000, but you had to get first class results for hatchability. We had four and a half thousand birds here and they came twice a week from Craven Arms to fetch the eggs, 18-20 thousand a week. The broilers could lay three thousand eggs a day, but they weren't all hatchable of course, there were cracked ones and mis-shapes. It was good money, but not without hard work, the important things were hygiene and attention to detail. I always used cod liver oil, we had it in 40 gallon drums and I put it on the mash with a squeezy bottle two or three times a week. I think it helped to get good strong chicks. We finished up with Dove Valley Poultry at Ashbourne and they used to put WOO on the boxes of our chicks and people would ask for them.

In between every batch of fresh poultry, we had to have a meticulous total scrub out, and the Ministry came to take sample swabs from everywhere, the ceiling, floor, nest boxes, fans etc. The ministry vet came to inspect monthly, except during foot and mouth in 1967/68. It was often Mr Bonallo; he'd go in the sheds with a torch on his head. When Granddad, Fred Woolley, had Fowl pest down near Biddulph, he was that worried in case I got it, especially as young John and Liz went there every day. In an old diary it says that on 2nd December 1963, Mr Bonallo came to inspect the breeding flock due to their chickens being exported from London Airport to Nigeria. They also went to Germany to take part in laying trials.

The job fitted in well with the cows; the lights came on at 3am, and at milking time at 5.30am, we collected eggs, then after breakfast, then again after dinner. At one time we had a problem with the cows and that year the poultry made more money. The shed is still like new, but we decided to give up when the increasing bureaucracy just got too much.

Ethel Bailey at Pyatts Barn.

Bill Oliver From an interview by Josie Hambleton and Ann Dowley 19/4/2001

I was born at Barleyford, yes, I am the only one left out of ten. School was quite all right. Our teachers were Mr Billy Banks and old Mrs Banks. Billy Banks was a very nice old fellow, but he got too old really. One of the Warburtons took the cane off him and thrashed him with it and then stuffed it down the lavatory. There were about ninety at school then.

Lots of snow; lot more than we have now. Yes, my mother and dad made us go school. There were drifts; walking through it this deep, there were no such thing as wellingtons in them days; boots or clogs, and tied bags round your legs.

I was 14 when I left school; I went out to service to my sister's at Sutton, farming. Then for Wilfred Eardley at Thompson Farm and then I left there and went droving for Len Mason, taking cows to Leek every Wednesday, starting at Minn End about 7 or 8 o'clock in the morning and gathering cows up all the way to Leek. There'd be 40 or 50 when we landed at Leek. Farmers would bring them down and meet us and we'd take them to the cattle market in Heywood Street . Occasionally we'd bring some back in the dark. I drove for quite a few years then went back to Wilfred Eardley's.

I plucked 100 chickens, geese and turkeys at Christmas, all on my own one year, the lad left just before Christmas. We had 200 hens and we used to sell eggs. Quite a good many years after I was married, I'd go to Leek on the 10 o'clock train to sell eggs and produce; I didn't have a car then. I took rabbits; very popular in those days. Ken Goodfellow and Sid Bullock used to come every Monday and we went ferreting. I took the rabbits to Leek; it was no trouble to sell them - they were waiting for you as you went in, one pulling you one side and t'other pulling you at the other side.

We had 36 cows, all milk, and took it to the station on horse and float. We did haymaking with horses, yes, me dad got killed with one at Barleyford; breaking one in. We had a proper breaking ring. Two of our horses went to the First World War. They came and took 'em; they didn't say you had got to send 'em, they came and took them, no matter what you said.

Never had a day off, couldn't afford, never had any spare time. Always gone dancing though. I think they were happier days than today though, I do.

RUSHTON & CLOUD END.

Woodwork class 1920s.

Christine Sale

Granny and granddad Baddiley farmed at Leaside, near Barnslea. When mother had children, I used to stop with them and walk to school from there. Then we lived at Fold Cottage, a little one up-one down near the Crown. Dad was a farmworker for Tommy Kirk at Brandylea.

There were quite a few children round there at Rushton James; we played with the Harrisons, Christine, Gordon and Malcolm; the Gibsons, Sheila, Janet and Kenny; Ann and Keith Dowley, Graham Beswick and Elizabeth Brassington. We made stilts out of milk cans and bag string. We went paddling down in the Dingle brook and got frogspawn and put it in jars.

I remember going on Chapel Walking Round Sundays. That was the last two Sundays in July. The first Sunday in August was the Anniversary. We met at the chapel, there'd be 25-30 of us and the band, and we'd walk round the houses and farms. We sang a couple of hymns at each place and then they gave us a donation, a bit like summer carol singing. At some places there were refreshments. At Harrisons we sat on forms in the orchard and Mrs Harrison gave us homemade ginger beer and biscuits; it was lovely.

When my grandparents retired, they moved to Marl Sprink with Uncle Frank. Mum lived at Heaton then and she walked from there to Marl Sprink once or twice a week for twenty years carrying shopping and washing. She called on me, here at Charles Knowle, on the way and one day when it was icy, she came back with a broken wrist.

The Hanging Gate pub was next door to us, I remember a 'Cherry B' was 1s 6d when we used to go in there regular. Annie Snelson and Hilda Gibson kept it. Friday nights were popular; when Roland was on afternoon shift at Adam's Butter he couldn't get the car in, it was that busy. Ernest Ash, a cattle dealer from Mossley came and Horace Pointon, who sold Nissen huts. There was always a nice fire and you could sit in their own front room if you wanted to. It closed in 1972.

The Robin Hood.

At the Hanging Gate.

Walking Sunday 1940s.

Bernard Brown

I was born in Rushton in 1931 at Ashlea; then we moved to Ventnor in Tan House Lane, then when I was twelve, we moved to The Limes down Station Lane to look after Mrs Hine. Dad had been her chauffeur and gardener and she said she'd commit suicide if he didn't go and look after her; throw herself under a train or into the millpond. We stayed until Mrs Hine died.

Then we went to Harpurs Farm for a short while, then Hall House Cottage near the station, then up to Glenroy till I got married. I've lived locally all my life except for my two years National Service, which I spent at Lichfield as clerk to the second in command.

Dad was born and brought up at Cloudside Farm. With his mates, they used to fetch pigeons' eggs off the Cloud. Dad was smallest, so they tied a rope round his waist, then dangled him over the edge and swung him about a bit till he could reach them. Then they cracked them and swallowed them raw.

Our parents took us to chapel until we were old enough to go to Sunday school; then it was Sunday school 10.30 'til 11, chapel 11 'til 12, Sunday school 2 'til 3 and chapel again from 6.30 till anytime up to 8.30, depending who was preaching. Even when I was in the Army, I visited home most weekends and went to chapel morning and night. If the sermon looked like being a long one, I had my bag ready on the pew at the side of me and when it got to 8 o'clock, I ran down and caught the bus to Leek, then another to Hanley, then another to Lichfield.

I always remember one old preacher telling the Christmas story about Joseph and Mary fleeing to Egypt to us children, *"Dun yo know yo lads what King Herod did to o' the babies in Bethle'em and rind abite?"* We all said, *"No."* *"Well I'll tell yer; ay knocked 'em i' th' neck!"*

On Walking Round Sunday, after we'd been to Rushton James, it was back to Chapel, where Mrs Needham from Overhouses and Mrs Harrison had prepared lunch; a good salad, perhaps ham, then cold custard and a pie, apple, rhubarb or gooseberry. It did taste good after walking round, very refreshing and a bit of luxury at the end of the war when there were lots of things you couldn't get. The next Sunday, there was herb beer and biscuits at Lizzie and Fanny Cave's.

At school in war time, Mr Banks had a whistle made out of a valve cap off a tyre and he blew across it. If that blew, it meant that there was some emergency and we had to dive under the hedges of the schoolyard. One day he blew it and we all dived under the hedge. A German plane came over, just above the height of the school. We saw the cross on the side, and could see the pilot and he waved to us. The planes often flew low over Rushton because there was an anti-aircraft gun up on Bosley Minn End and it couldn't tilt down enough to shoot at them if they were low, as they were going over to bomb Manchester and Liverpool. You sometimes saw puffs of white smoke where anti-aircraft shells were exploding round them.

Dad was in the A.R.P. during the war and this involved sleeping in a wooden hut where Hallam's garage is now. One of our duties as children was to sweep out and tidy the hut where the wardens slept. When the evacuees came from Manchester, they went to school in the morning and we went in the afternoon, then the next week it was opposite for a while until they went back. They were full of mischief and always wanted to fight. One called Theresa Saunders stayed with us. If you upset her she'd say, *"I'll bash your eye in!"* One day we took her up the road for a walk and stopped at the pump at the garage. She said, *"We've got one of these, I'll show you how it works."* She picked it up and shot petrol across the road.

Norman Parton came out and snatched it off her.

Afterwards, the boy we had from London, Eric, was the opposite, very polite. He stayed for three years until the end of the war. One day we were in Leek when word got out that they had jellies for sale in Woolworths. The allocation was one per person, so mother, Eric and I joined the queue which stretched out along Derby Street; and after a long wait we each got a jelly. When we got home, mother said, *"Show dad what we got in Leek today."* And we put our jellies on the table; but there were only two. *"Where is yours, Eric?"* Mother asked. *"I'm sorry Madam,"* he replied. *"I've eaten mine."* He was sick and no-one felt sorry for him.

I also remember mother queuing in Leek for several hours for her first ever pair of nylons. They lasted for years; no other nylons lasted anything like as long as her first pair.

As we got older and got cars, a group of us lads would travel round after chapel to see who was coming out of some of the other chapels, like Cloud chapel, Biddulph Moor or Key Green. I suppose we were looking for 'respectable' girls. John Heathcote had a car, Reg Beswick and Bill Wood too, and John Harvey and I had vans. I actually met my wife at a dance at Cauldon Lowe. I'd gone with John Heathcote and when we got there, there was no-one there and they wanted half-a-crown to get in; it was usually two shillings. We said to the chap on the door, *"Is there anyone else coming?" "Yes, come on in lads, come in." "Are there any women up here?" "Oh, ah, plenty women." "Are they any good?" "Oh, they're alright."* But we wouldn't go in because it was half-a-crown. Then an A40 van pulled in. *"The's some comin' now, some in theer."* A girl got out and went round the back of the van and let three more out. We said, *"Are*

they all as good as these?" "Oh, ah, theer all nice up 'ere." So we paid up and went in. And when we got dancing, the first thing that I found out was that she went to chapel. Come home time, and we offered to take them home. When we said we'd got a van, they thought that would be alright, they'd all fit in. But when we came to load up and I'd got a spray of ether 'aerostart', and a sofa in the back, they were frightened to death. But they got over it and my wife and I have never looked back since.

Since then, I've taught at Brown Edge School for 13 years. That was general teaching, juniors and it's since closed. I was headteacher at Sheen for twelve and a half years; that's closed. Head at Swythamley for one year; that's closed. And my last five years were at Blackshaw Moor, the only one still open yet!

In 1958, I bought a 45 seater coach and at weekends, some evenings and in the holidays, I drove that. When I finished that, I drove wagons for Moss and Lovatt for a while delivering concrete pipes.

We are proud of our Primitive Methodist connections and when Ramsor chapel was closed, we bought it, and have held special services, which have always been well supported.

Back: Ernest Malkin, Don Davies, Ron Goodfellow, John Pickford, Harold Dale.
:Derek Trueman, George Slack, Joe Findler, Phillip Gibson, Les Goodwin, Stanley Lovatt, Johnty Knight, Donald Holland
Front: Harold Banks, Headmaster, Peter Robinson, Norman Rogers, Herbert Coates, Reg Brown, Michael Holland.

Back: Ralph Steele, Bob Torr, P. Boon, Tom Needham, Jim Pyatt.
2nd: Jim Eardley, Frank Brown, Jack Brough, Robert Needham, Arnold Turnock, Mr Barks Snr
:Jack Sumner (drum), Wilf Gibson, Dick Oliver, Tom Cotterill, Frank Twigg, John Eardley, Harry Twigg, Sidney Warburton
Front: Merrill Wayne, Jim Goodfellow, Edgar Robinson, Jack Moss.

Eva Oliver

Taken from an interview by Josie Hambleton and Ann Dowley. 1/5/2001.

I was born at Pyatt's Barn, Hilda was too, but I don't think Annie or Ethel were. My father died when he was 48; mother and Annie did the milking then. We used to go to Biddulph Park chapel on a Sunday; walk there and back of course.

We went to Rushton School and came down as far as Rushton Hall on the milk float that was taking our milk to the station. At Rushton Hall we met Ethel Bowler and walked the rest of the way.

My sister Ethel was working at Pooles Café in Leek when she got scarlet fever, she was 21. She had it very bad and was taken to the isolation hospital at Tinsterwood. You were just shut in a hospital in those days, no visitors like there is today. I'd be about 7 and only got it slightly, but I can remember it very well. Hilda got it slightly as well. Mother wouldn't let them take me into hospital; she had to stay with me in the one room for weeks. Ethel got rheumatoid arthritis after that and never worked again. Annie had to go out to work after that.

When the farm was sold, we came to live at the Woodlands in Alley Lane. I was 9 and that same year, I was the Well Dressing Queen. We started to go to Rushton Church. Choir men and boys sat in the choir stalls and the choir girls sat in the Swythamley pews.

I left school at 14 and went to work at Wilson's hat shop in Leek. I went there on the 8 o'clock train. I had Thursday afternoons off, and worked all day Saturday. I worked there for four years and got six shillings a week and had to pay train and bus fares out of that.

After that I went to Percy Bailey's in Derby Street; it was a well-stocked shop. It closed at 6 o'clock, but if you'd got a customer, you couldn't just leave them. I've chased my legs off to catch that 7 o'clock train and when you got there, it was just going out; so I didn't get back till the 9.15 pm bus; sometimes I stayed at Annie's. Then Percy Bailey's dissolved partnership and I went to work at Emmie Bailey's. I worked the same hours but got more money. Then when war broke out, I had to move again, to Daimler.

You hadn't time to go out socially, by the time you had got buses and trains, there wasn't time. There was no electric, no water, nothing. We used rainwater for washing. Mother took in holidaymakers for weekends; I would be in my teens. They came to walk in the Dane Valley and around.

OPPOSITE PAGE:
TOP:
Back: Maurice Goodwin, John Simpson, Norman Cope, Albert Goldstraw
2nd: Frank Baddiley, Doris Coates, Marjorie Corden, Lily Heathcote,
Edith Cantrill, Elaine Davenport, Miss Elsie Simpson
3rd: Norman Edwards, Hilda Barker, Irene Lovatt, Beryl Cope,
Dorothy Knowles, Ernest Rogers
Front: Arthur Grimwood, David Gibson, Bill Wood, Bernard Brown,
Cyril Edwards, Brian Eardley, Malcolm Bowyer

BOTTOM:
1930s. Eva Bailey, Michael Holland, Norman Rogers,
John Pickford, Ron Goodfellow, Don Davies, Reg Brown, Dennis Eardley.

Early 1900s.

Peter Jones

I was born in Dover, moved to London when I was three or four, and after grammar school came to N.W. England serving an apprenticeship with the Oil Well Engineering Company in Cheadle Heath, near Stockport. My idea was to go abroad as my elder brother was working in Persia; however before my apprenticeship finished, I was offered a job at Gun Hill. D'Arcy Exploration Company, a subsidiary of Anglo Persian Oil Co, later B.P. were exploring all over England then and had this rig on Gun Hill. So I joined them in September 1938, I was twenty.

It was very rough country in those days; bog and moorland. The only way onto the site was on tracks of railway sleepers and they just sank into the bog, so they were re-laid, sleepers on top of sleepers to keep access. The equipment was very heavy, enormous Allen diesel engines and massive iron mud-pumps, which were necessary in order to pump fluid mud through the drill string at very high pressure to cool the rockbit and lift the cuttings to surface. An even more important function of the mud was to have sufficient weight to counteract the possibility of a blowout due to meeting unexpected high pressure gas or oil. The pressures you get under ground are enormous, for example, 2000 psi; water wouldn't hold against it, you have to weight up the water with clay and barytes to make the mud.

There was a big tank of mud and it was circulated up through a rotating swivel which held the drill pipe, down through the pipe, then up through the space between the outside of the pipe and the wall to the surface and the circulating tank. The cuttings came out over a vibrating screen; you could see what formation you were going through. It was vital to have a man on that tank to watch the level of the mud; it should remain constant unless you hit a large cavity in the formation, when you start to lose mud. As soon as he saw that, he'd tell the driller quick and they brought in extra mud; there was a 40 foot long mud tank in reserve. You had to have plenty in case you had rapid loss; if you couldn't cope, gas could cause a blow out.

The drilling rig itself was 136 feet high, with four legs on big solid concrete foundations. 4,500 feet of $4^1/2$ inch drill pipe with collars could weigh as much as 35-40 tons and extra power could be required at times to free the drill string if it became stuck. The lifting tackle required a travelling pulley block of ten sheaves and strung with 8-10 lines of 1 inch wire line. It's not been unknown for people to pull the derrick in on them; there are terrific forces involved.

The operation ran day and night on a three shift system; 8 till 4, 4 till midnight and midnight till 8. Every weekend it was shut down and the shifts changed around to vary it. That was in the soft days - they never shut down after that.

There was a derrick man on the 'fourble' platform, 80 feet high. There's a history in that. In the old days they used 4 x 20ft lengths of drill pipe; 80ft, that was called a fourble. We used trebles, 3 x 30ft in one stand. When you pull out of the hole, you pull the pipe up to 90ft, wedge it at the bottom and unscrew a 90ft length of pipe. A man on the floor pulls it round into a rack, then the derrick man has to gather the top loose end and stack it in the corner of the derrick. Working up there, 80ft up in the air, on top of Gun Hill in winter wasn't a job many fancied. Each shift had its own derrick man; they got a little extra pay, but they earned it.

The number of people employed was quite large, they were mostly from Leek, a lorry used to bring them up. There were 3 shifts of 8 or 9 men; derrick man, pump man, roustabouts on shift work, plus daytime staff of a manager, Bob Roberts, accountant, storekeeper, also a blacksmith, Bob, and Geoff, a maintenance engineer who had come from

Portsdown in Hampshire, where the rig had drilled before without success.

There was a man, Dudeney, who had worked in Peru and the oilfields of South America. He was storekeeper cum first aid man. He and his wife lived in a small caravan in a small quarry opposite White Shaw all winter. How she stood it, I don't know. His first aid was rough but effective.

At Christmas time, Bob Roberts, the tool-pusher, whether it was economy or carelessness, omitted to change the cooling water in the engines to anti-freeze or glycerine, as they did in those days. There were drums of it in store; we didn't realise until afterwards. So we shut down for Christmas and it froze and froze. When we came back, it was 14 days before

we got going again. The cooling jackets were split, the pumps were split, the damage was dreadful.

One of the drillers was called Alan Rutherford; he was a New Zealander and the nephew of Lord Rutherford, the atomic scientist. He lodged in Leek at the White Swan. And there was a Scottish driller, Alec Fife. When the shifts were right, on a Wednesday night I used to have a meal with them, then we'd go off to Hanley to see the all-in wrestling. There was a man called Jim, who used to walk from Flash, day or night, no matter what the weather. He used to bring a rabbit or two and sell them for 6d each; he set snares on his way to and from work.

Another unforgettable character was a French Canadian driller, Louis Berchant. He stayed at The Golden Lion in Rushton. He liked a tipple and drove a big Citroen. Of course, the inevitable happened; he wrapped it round a telegraph pole one night and was injured. He was a rough character with a rough accent, almost illiterate, but had enormous experience.

I stayed at Butley Town, near Prestbury and commuted. As an apprentice, I was earning 7s 6d a week and when I joined the oil company, it went up to £4 10s; that was money! I went straight into Quicks in Manchester and bought a Ford car on HP for £25.

In late February, we'd gone down four and a half thousand feet, when we got quite a flow of fresh water. We realised there was no point in going any further, so abandoned the well, cemented it to surface and moved to near Nottingham, where they actually struck oil. It was the first productive oil well in England at that time. The day they started drilling there though, I left to go to Persia.

I was a 'roughneck' - a trainee driller. I finished as a driller, my last job was superintendent driller in Iraq in 1956. I then joined the Hughes Tool Company. Howard Hughes's father had started the company to manufacture rock drilling bits and the profits helped Howard Hughes to form his own private airline, the famous Trans World Airline, TWA, along with his film ventures. I joined the London office as a sales rep, travelling the Middle East and Africa for them. Working out there in the summertime, temperatures could reach 130 odd degrees, terribly hot. My mind often slipped back to that cold winter up on Gun Hill.

Mona Edwards

My maternal grandad Massey lived at Spring Bank, Dial Lane. He was the youngest of a big family and worked in a pit at Biddulph. He also used to do pig-killing. Thompsons at Bosley Mill kept a lot of pigs and he was often doing for them. Later on, he farmed at The Lee, then moved to Intakes Farm. He retired when he was 50 and built the bungalow up there, now known as The Mount.

I've never lived anywhere but Rushton. I was born at The Millhouse. Father, Sam Moss ran the corn mill; he rented it off Mr Lockitt. Before that, he'd worked at the mill with Mr Brown, who had lived at the Millhouse before. There were two millponds and we couldn't swim, but we came to no harm. We lived in the brooks and the village lads came down playing; trying to jump the brooks, climbing over hencote roofs, all sorts of things.

I went to stay with my Aunt Annie three nights a week and I'd go with her to visit old Polly Sumner up Sugar Street. When you were children then, you didn't say anything; you just sat and listened to the old folks talking. She was a character, very rough spoken, but did a lot of lovely crocheting. She always wore a lace cap and worked by candlelight.

Mrs Moss at the Millhouse, 1930.

Father ran a little wagon in the early 1920s and when the railways went on strike in 1926, mother said to him, *"Why don't you approach the farmers and offer to take the milk to Manchester for them?"* They sold their own milk then and would have to pay carriage. He soon got a round big enough for a full load. Then Mr Cook, at the Dyehouse Mill asked him to bring corn back from Manchester for them. Sam Lovatt, from Biddulph Moor worked for him, and in 1928, he became a partner and they expanded the business. The farmers paid their own haulage until 1933, when the Milk Marketing Board was formed. They then organised the rounds and contracted to pay us.

The business grew, we hauled all sorts of stuff, then in 1949, haulage firms over a certain size were nationalised into British Road Services. So it was decided to split the running of the business; mother and father ran the milk and corn side as Moss and Lovatt and Mr and Mrs Lovatt concentrated on the long distance haulage, calling that, Rushton Spencer Transport. BRS was de-nationalised in 1954 and we bought several of their wagons then; bringing us up to 24 wagons.

Mr Brown and Mr Moss are in this photo at Rushton Mill in the 1930s.

Stan Lovatt and Les Cope, late 1940s.

After leaving school, I went to work at Wardle and Davenports in Leek in the office. But town life didn't suit me, I was often ill. There were no proper dinners and I was a bit nervy. And the trains home, if you just missed one, it was nearly 7 when you got home. It was wartime and there were planes coming over, they used to follow the trains; you were scared of being bombed. The carriages were blacked out, you didn't know who you were getting in with; there was just a faint little bulb sometimes. It wasn't very nice; I used to run like mad across Mill Lane when I got off the train. So when Mr Cook wanted some help at the mill, I was glad to go there, though I'd got on well with them at Wardle and Davenports, they didn't want me to leave.

At Cook's, I had to help with the accounts and there was the extra work with the rationing coupons; piles of them and each one had to be written on. If a farmer brought them in, Mr Cook wrote on the top one, whose they were and I had to fill the rest in. There were always farmers coming and going; one used to shout me out to hold his horse. Another one, I think he was called Wainwright, used to come down the Feeder side with his horse and put a couple of bags on the horse's back and went along.

I met Stanley at Chapel youth club. I was also learning to play the organ and had to pay a lad to pump for me, the electric blower wasn't put in until the mid-50s. So when Stan pumped for me, I didn't pay him! But later he got me back when I was practising once; they tied the chapel door up and fastened me in.

I carried on at Cook's part-time after we were married, mother looked after the children. I was always among the Moss and Lovatt business and when my parents retired, I went in with my brother Victor; he used to drive as well. I was made a director in 1968. Sam Lovatt's son Stanley was in too, he worked in the garage. His second son, Geoff retired last year and our sons, David and Nigel run the business now.

Early 1950s.

Stan Edwards

My father was a road man; he drove a steamroller and carried on till he was seventy. In his early days, he did steam ploughing. He started off working for Jackson's of Wistaston near Crewe, then got to working for the council. When I was a child, we lived for a while at Warslow, where if we were naughty, mum locked us in the police cell and you didn't get out till she let you out. Then we lived for a while at Ecton before moving to Heaton when I was about seven. We lived at The Black Horse, which was then a little cottage after having been a pub. It felt very small as there were eight of us. We were often playing pranks and always got the blame for things, but we usually had some help. Like the time the gates in the village were swapped round one night.

Dad had to go where the work was, so he lived in a little van with iron-tyred wheels which was towed behind the steam roller. He went off on his bike on a Monday morning, with a basket of groceries and came back Saturday. He lived on his own in the van.

When he was working in our area, he'd let us steer the engine. It felt great up there, but you had to work, wizzling the wheel round.

During the war, Michelin in Stoke used to do tyre-testing up around Flash. They had vehicles belting up and down testing tyres for endurance and it chewed the side roads up. So the council had to put stone down and dad had to level and roll it.

When I left school I went working at the timber dump. Evans and Bellhouse stored their timber out at Rushton during the war because of the bombing in Manchester. From the River Dane to the village, the fields both sides of the road were one big row of stacks of sawn planks. Most of it was white wood, but the field next to Lane End farm was stacked full of cedar wood and they built a big open shed to cover that. All the timber came by rail, the foreign timber from Liverpool Docks. My job was to check it off a list as it was unloaded from a railway wagon onto a bogey truck. What boat it had come off, what type

Logging at Barleyford 1942/43.
Tom Sumner, George Oliver on tractor and Fred Wainwright. All felled by hand-axe and saw.

On Gratton-Endon road.

of timber it was and the length.

There was a little tractor thing running the timber backwards and forwards all the time. It was all moved by hand, a lot of the workmen came from Manchester, some lived out here. It was stacked out here for safety and as they needed it, they fetched it on lorries. The same firm took a lot of timber out of Barleyford and Back Dane. That was pulled out with a steam wagon. A lot of locals worked for them as well. The men who did the stacking came from Manchester; when the stacks got high, they made a zig-zag runway to walk up. They had a leather pad on their shoulders and waxed it, so the wood just slid off and the stacker put it into place. The stacks were as high as house roofs. They knew their jobs.

I stopped there 12 months, then went as mate on a wagon with Albert Trueman - him and Mr Brassington had a lorry each. We worked out of Wood Treatment at Bosley, taking wood flour out and bringing shavings and sawdust back. I was dogsbody, help to load and sheet up, grease monkey and clean the wagon. We left Rushton at 5 o'clock every morning for Birmingham; it was a three hour journey then.

I left there and went to Robinson's wheelwrights and joiners, for three or four years general labouring. Jobs like digging holes for haysheds by hand, helping the blacksmith and going down wells. I must have been down most of them in the area; the Golden Lion regularly. It was to fix the pumps; a lot of them were down the wells; the leather washers got hard or worn out. The clack on the lift made a groove and if the leather went hard, it let the water back. So we either had to soften them and put them back or put a new one in. You often got a stone slab and a drop of warm water and rubbed the leather on it to soften, then it could go back. I'd also cut timber down and fetch it in.

Then it was back on the wagons with Mr Brassington at Glenroy; Mr Trueman had packed up then. I learnt to drive with him. We fetched shavings in bags from sawmills, a lot out of Burton-on-Trent. They were hundredweights; an eight ton load was 160 bags, all loaded by hand. That was till 1950, when I came to Moss and Lovatt shifting milk and corn.

My first round was around Rushton James and Biddulph Park, maybe twenty pick-ups, then take it into Manchester. Mainly to one dairy, some drivers had to go to three. Mayfair Sterilized only took three loads. We went to Heald's at Didsbury, then Express at Wythenshawe and the Co-op at Holden Bridge.

I unloaded on my own, bowling them off onto the conveyor; twelve gallon churns mainly then. It was a double deck, thrown on by hand often with a bit of help from the farmers. After loading the empties back onto the lorry, it was off to the corn mills, one,

sometimes two and we put 5 or 6 ton of corn, in hundredweight bags, on top of the empty churns. There was bran, flaked maize, compounds, hen corn, all sorts, in hessian sacks. You backed along the side of the chute and you were running about on top of the milk churns with hob-nailed boots on; you had to watch the bags coming down the chute, that they didn't knock you over.

When you got back, some of the corn was delivered to farmers; a lot went into Cook's mill. You started between 7.30 and 8 in the morning and finished when you finished, often 9 o'clock at night. The hours didn't count in them days. That was 7 days a week, no corn on Saturdays and Sundays. No time off, no Bank holidays or Christmas day. I didn't have a Christmas day off in 13 or 14 years.

There was a race on between wagons, to get in the Dairy queue. At Heald's, at 11 o'clock, there might be 8 or 10 wagons in front of you. You could have your butties then. I've had one or two races down Kingsway.

In snow, the farmers came to meet you, perhaps with horse and cart and the churns on, which they'd back up to you. We used to have to do a lot of digging. You could be picking milk up

1967.

all day. Mona came with me one night; we took a double load. 112 x 12 gallon churns and 91 on top; some churns over full, we hadn't been to the farms for three days. There were 30 or 40 at one place. They had to keep a few spare empties about. It was a young man's job, I wouldn't like to do it nowadays.

Bartram and Holland started the same time as us, and they had about 10 wagons, the same as us. Our phone number was 9, theirs was 10. On the back of their wagons it said, *"Ring Rushton 10, We'll shift it."* There was a friendly rivalry, if a Moss and Lovatt wagon met a Bartram and Holland wagon on a narrow lane, they'd argue as to who had to back up. They sold out to Cartwright and Jackson, a milk firm who got nationalised. Then when British Road services were de-nationalised in the 1950s, Sam Holland bought some of the wagons and started Mason's Garage at Bosley.

When churns were being phased out, we looked at milk tankers, but decided to give the milk job up and increase the general haulage side. We finished churns on December 31st 1977. We shift a lot of concrete now for people. And we work with a crane hire firm in the Potteries, who lift barges out of canals and we move them about.

W.I. 1960s.

W.I. Concert 1950s.

Herbert Harrison

I was born in 1914 at Brook Farm. We moved to New Hall Farm in March 1917. Both farms were part of the Antrobus Estate. Mr Antrobus had said to father about moving, *"Harrison, do you think you can manage it?"* It was 77 acres and in 1920, the rent was £115. He bought the farm in 1926, when it was offered for sale. It cost £1,600. I just remember walking behind the trap as they were flitting to New Hall. Until the farm was purchased, mother, father and I were invited annually to Eaton Hall as guests of Mr Antrobus, for a day out. We went in the pony and trap via Havannah Lane, Buglawton.

I had my tonsils out on the kitchen table. Dr Somerville came and put his case on the table and said, *"Get on the table, we'll have them out."* I wasn't much age. *"Tell your mother to go for a walk as far as Rushton Station and they'll be out."*

I had an iron hoop and a stick, I called it my bowler; we've still got it somewhere. And I played marbles in the road at Lane End Farm, where my grandparents lived. I went across in the school dinner hour, playing with Jimmy Salt. They brought him up when his parents died. Tramps would sometimes stay there overnight, on the way to Leek Workhouse. Granny, who was a midwife, made them leave their pipes on a ledge till the next day, then they could sleep in the hayshed.

Mother, Dora, would walk to Congleton with butter to sell. Father, John, mowed the golf course at Cliffe Park.

There were two wells in Rushton James; people fetched water with yokes until 1970s. I can remember a servant maid at Rushton Hall was fetching water all the time and wore out clog tips every two or three weeks. I knew Dingle Lane as To' Bar Lane. Originally there was a toll bar at the Crown Inn in 1805. Then one at Ryecroft Gate in 1820. It was taken off in 1876.

When we went to school, we ran down the fields, crossed the railway, then another field and if the bell had stopped ringing, you knew you were late. Charlie Woodward, from Oxhay was with me; he had even further to walk. I played a euphonium in Rushton band and when I was learning, as a teenager, I had to walk through the fields to Barnslea with a little lantern and my instrument, to have lessons with Mr Corbishley. We had band practice in the garage at New Hall. Tom Beswick played E flat, Walter Hulme, tenor horn and Arthur Needham, slide trombone.

When I was 17, I went on trial to be a local preacher. I walked miles or cycled to chapels. A group of us once cycled to Cliff College at Calver for the anniversary celebrations and my bike broke down - the old Sunbeam is still up in the granary. Later on I went regularly on the Sunday with my parents and on Whit Monday took our children. I served the Leek and Congleton Methodist circuits for over 60 yrs as a local preacher.

I spent 43 yrs in local government and stepped down when I was 80. I was councillor for Rushton, Horton and Longsdon. One of my biggest fights was in the 1970s. There was a proposal to raise Rudyard Lake by 75 feet, which would mean a dam of 75 feet at Ryecroft Gate. They wanted to pump water from the Dane into it and it was not going to be used for this district but for Winsford.

James Arthur Gibson of Ryecroft used to keep a pet water otter and would show off to visitors the shed where it was kept; telling them to get hold of a stick, it was savage with young ones. It was tied onto a chain. Then he pulled the chain out of the shed, and out it came. It was a kettle!

Early 1960s Parish Council. L to R.
Winifred Moss, Wilfrid Gibson, Alice Dale, Rev. Frank Sutton, Herbert Harrison, William Gibson,
John Lockitt, Harry Corbishley, Winnie Oliver, George Oliver.

1922. Pipe Band. Herbert is 4th from the left, back row.

Gordon Harrison

Mr Banks was our school teacher. He always liked us to salute him; he'd been in the army and told army stories and when the Attendance Officer came, he got us to line up and salute him. He took snuff and wore spats; and when he was driving, he put a pad around his belly to stop his suit getting shiny. If we were naughty, he'd say, *"Get Uncle Peter out of the drawer."* And we knew what was coming, it was the cane!

During my lifetime, the only person that I knew to use the parish title, Rushton James, was Mr Banks. It was amalgamated with Rushton Spencer in 1934. If there was snow, he used to say, *"All the Rushton James children line up here"*. He put an oldest child at the front and back and sent us home. These last few years, the Post has started using the title again.

Walking home from school, we passed Bill Holland's pig farm. He kept a big white Alsatian and us children used to think it was half-wolf. It could jump as high as the wall and we tried to get past it before it knew we were there, but we never did. Walking further to the Hanging Gate, we used to stop and watch Vic Buckley making anything from wood; even coffins, when we knew then somebody local had died. Going to school sometimes you'd see tramps asleep on the Feeder side; steam would be rising off them.

We were always a big chapel family; dad often got up at 5am to have a go at getting sermons ready before milking. He used to say that grandad started hand-milking on a Sunday afternoon at 2.30 so he'd be done for chapel.

Dad had a Zephyr car at one time and when he was washing the milking machine on a Sunday morning, he'd back it out of the garage, open the windows and turn the radio up to listen to the morning service.

Mum was always helping out on the catering side. And I remember on Walking Sunday, when we got round to Cook's mill and everyone went on across to the Lee, I stayed behind and had a boat ride on the mill pond with John Cook.

Church Church Fête helpers in the 1950s.
Back: Josephine Yardley, Alice Dale, Ethel Goodfellow, Phyllis Allen, Annie Holland, Hilda Buckley, --, Eva Oliver, Lily Davenport, Maggie Condliffe, May Barlow, Florence Atkinson, Phyllis Warren, Elsie Banks, Minnie Buckley, Mrs Robinson
Front: Dolly Preston, Joan Allen, Eileen Steele, Muriel Malkin, Florence Chadwick, Selina (Ena) Lockitt, Mrs Cooper.

Wedding of Harriet Dale and James Turnock, 30th June 1909.

Mabel Goodfellow

I was born in 1919 at Wormhill Farm. My grandad was William Dale. When he got married, they lived at The Anthony and had four children, John, Fred, Arthur and Harriet. Then they moved to Rushton cottage, where mother and Uncle Percy were born. He'd been in the army, in the Guards; where they slept on beds more like a table top than anything else to keep them straight. He wouldn't have any sluggishness, if he saw you slouching, he threatened to put a broomstick between your shoulder blades. He was straight as a ramrod till the end when he died at 94.

Grandad Dale.

When he came out of the army, he trained to be a tailor. He worked at home, sitting cross-legged making men's suits. He had a sewing machine. I've still got a patch work of tailors samples of his that he used to put on the bed. But he needed extra money, so he became a postman to get a weekly wage, such as it was then. The round started at the station, went up into Heaton and Swythamley and finished at Wildboarclough. Then he'd got to walk back. He called at Swythamley Hall and was friendly with old Sir Philip. One day they were discussing the size of the round and Sir Philip said, *"Dale, I'll give you a donkey."* The next time he saw him, he asked, *"Dale where's the donkey?"* Grandfather replied, *"In my pocket."* You couldn't take a donkey over stiles and through brooks.

When he finished, Sir Philip had a huge cup and saucer made with his name in gilt on it. He was presented with it and treasured it. He was also awarded the Imperial Service Medal for his work as an officer in the postal service. *"Mr Dale joined the service in 1872 and it is calculated that up until the time of his retirement in December 1907, he had walked upwards of 197,600 miles in the discharge of his duties."*

Grandma was a Tunnicliffe, related to the artist, one of thirteen born at Feeder Cottage. For a time, she was a midwife and also laid people out. She 'hatched and despatched'; so between her and grandad, they knew everything that was going on in the area.

Aunt Harriet got an apprenticeship and went to work at Whaley Bridge in a bakery for seven years. Her wage was half-a-crown at Christmas and they had to go to Chapel on Sunday - they were given 6d to put in the collection. When you became fully qualified in those days you could not set up business within seven miles of where you learned your trade. You signed to that, so Rushton would be far enough away for her to set up business, which she did. They built the shop and bakehouse onto Alley House on Sugar Street. She had married James Turnock; he was a clerk, working at Biddulph and District. Then he had

Tenants' Hall, Swythamley.

From right to left, Uncle Sidney Chappell, Ruth, Stan and Sid Jnr at Buglawton.

an accident and broke his knee. He wouldn't have it mended, so he always walked with a limp after. So he looked after the shop, selling bacon, groceries, sweets and doing office work. And Aunt Harriet did the bakehouse.

She had a coke oven, Sam Lovatt brought the coke. She employed four girls, and everything had to be done by hand, there was no electricity. All the bread had to be kneaded, so they had to take it in turns. She sold a 2lb loaf, which had to be weighed out at 2lb 2oz because of the shrinkage, for 4¹/₂d. Someone asked her, *"Why is your bread a ha'penny dearer than anyone else's?"* She replied, *"Because my bread is made with milk."* It was hard work, but she did very well indeed. When they were extremely busy, I went to help out if I could be spared.

She charged 2s 6d per guest for weddings. There would be boiled ham, boiled tongue, roast beef, bread and butter, pickles and chutneys, all home-made, trifles and jellies. The bride's parents had to supply the drink and the wedding cake was extra. You could have a real fill up, plenty of everything. That was the 1930s, usually in the chapel room or the school room.

We catered at Swythamley Hall for the Tenant's dinner and the Primrose League garden party. I helped in the kitchen up there, unpacking dishes, washing up, dishing up; we had to make sure that the cutlery was spot on. The younger Sir Philip was friendly with Aunt Harriet and sent his chauffeur, Michael down to the bakeshop on a Friday for confectionary.

Mincemeat and lemon curd were made on the premises. The butter came in bulk, in big wooden tubs, never margarine, it was Danish. Sugar and flour by the hundredweight. Kilvert's lard in big slabs; she wouldn't use anything else. Local fresh eggs and milk from us. When it was coming up to winter and she thought eggs would be scarce, she'd buy extra and put them down in waterglass; good big buckets full in an outer place. She made Christmas cakes and puddings which she boiled up in the wash boiler.

Funerals were done at peoples houses, she charged 1s 6d per funeral guest, there were no trifles, currant bread instead. On Fridays, Messina Knowles, butcher from Leek used to bring meat for some of his customers and leave it at the shop. They paid their bills when they went to Leek the next Wednesday. Messina went back with swiss buns, swiss rolls and pork pies. Uncle Jim went shopping on Wednesday and brought a lot of pork back.

She made the pork pies on Thursdays. When I was at school, you could have a pork pie for 4d and a packet of crisps for 2d. She made cocoa for the children in the break; the water at school wasn't fit to drink. Parents paid her 1d a cup.

When Sally Cook gave up the post office, I think about 1938, Aunt Harriet took that on as well and she had the switchboard in her front room. She had to do night duty in the war because the lines needed to be manned for the Observer Corps. That would be after uncle Jim died. She said she hardly got into bed properly and told someone that she hadn't had her corsets off for a while.

Before she was married, mother kept a shop next door to Rushton Cottage, selling all sorts of things. Being as everybody had to light a candle, lamp or fire, they sold a lot of matches. They were done in packets of twelve boxes and sold for 2d for the dozen.

Dad was born and bred at Bent End Farm, Buglawton; they later moved to Pecks

House, Rushton, where he met mother. John Turnock had farmed here at Wormhill and Uncle Gilbert married his daughter, Lizzie and they were here until they moved to Tithe Barn Farm, when dad and mother married and came here. At that time the farm was rented from a Mr Cresswick - dad bought it later. I was born in 1919, the third of four, but I lost my oldest brother when he was three. They said it was through eating tinned salmon

Drinking water was carried from a spring down the fields with buckets and yokes. When I left school, dad put a petrol engine and pump down there. There was a pond at the front and another at the back for the cattle and there was a well, and a pump in the dairy to draw water to cool the milk. This water then overflowed into a trough for the cows, when they were inside. And of course there were rain tubs; every bit of water was used carefully.

Dad grew potatoes, peas, beans, beetroot, turnips, carrots and cabbages for the family and mangolds and big ox-cabbage, oats and rye for the cattle. His parents had been great ones for growing crops. He wanted everything to be self supporting. There were about 16 cows, the calves were born in February, so the cows were milking, then got a boost when they went out in May. And there were some young stock following on.

Mother was a good cheese maker, she often won competitions and at the well dressing. It was a level dairy where dad sold the milk to and, same as at holiday times, they didn't want it, so they used to send a telegram boy from Danebridge post office through the fields to say keep your milk at home the next day or perhaps two days. So we made butter or cheese. We had a separator and fed the whey to the pigs. People knew we'd got it and always bought it, they knew mum was brought up to be clean, grandma was a stickler.

When I left school, I helped at home and went cleaning for grandad on a Friday. I did the calf feeding. When they had been on milk for a while, I made gruel for them. It was a mixture of linseed oilcake meal and bran mixed with cold water then boiling water put on and mixed up half and half with milk. They did do well on it, their coats shone. The oilcake made the barn floor slippy where the lickin' pile was. That was where you emptied your sacks of feed out in layers, bran, flaked maize, oats, pulped roots, whatever and then it was turned with big shovels to mix it.

One of the best things was seeing the chickens hatch, the little golden things, cheeping. Turnip thinning was very boring; but I think the worst job was tedding hay out after you'd hobbled it up if there came a thunderstorm.

Dad took the milk down to the station till the rail strike, then Bartram Holland picked it up from the end of the lane. They made a platform and milk was left there from Barleyford, Thompson and Brandylee as well. You hadn't to be late taking it down.

I took eggs to the Buttermarket in Leek. I went down the fields with big baskets of eggs to catch Findlow's bus at the bottom of Tan House Lane. It only ran on a Wednesday. This was in the '30s; I'd be 14 or 15. Dad went with me to start with, then he went off down to the cattle market. There were 13 dozen eggs in each basket, packed in chopped straw, which we'd cut with the chaffcutter. I once tripped getting over a stile and broke some; we salvaged what we could and made lemon cheese with them.

The bus dropped us off at the top of the market place, then we walked down to the Buttermarket entrance where you paid a toll, so much a dozen, I think, had your hand stamped and went in. Inside, you put your baskets on long trestles; you didn't know who you were going to be standing next to. Buyers would come and look at your eggs; *"No, I don't want them at that price."* If your eggs were clean and well presented, you hadn't much trouble to sell them. They knew if your eggs were good.

Some people had butter to sell and chickens were sold up in the top end. As soon as you sold up, you moved out, some came in later. Mrs Fernihough, from Heaton Lowe would be coming in as we came home. She'd have her regular customers. One time after Easter, I sold 40 dozen eggs and had 30 shillings. Father was ill, so I got him a few flowers, did all the shopping and still had change.

My brothers didn't go in the war, Gilbert went helping other farmers and father had a heart condition so even though Arthur was working at Robinsons, it was arranged that he did so many hours at home as well, so he milked before he went. Some bombs dropped in the wood one night and I remember a barrage balloon got stuck in a tree; it must have broken loose from somewhere.

In the house we had a Dutch oven, which fitted on the front of the range. You could put bacon or sausage on hooks and cook it over eggs. It was wonderful; the eggs were cooked to perfection. Electricity came to the farm in 1955 and mains water in 1963.

Going back to the Buttermarket, I remember one day two women standing next to me talking. One says, *"Eeh, 'ow's your Bill, I anner sayn 'im lately?"* *"Well,"* the other replied, *"If ay'd a lived till termerrer, ayd a bin d'yed a fortneet."*

Wedding of Florence Dale and Wilfred Chappell, 3rd January 1912.

Ron Goodfellow

The Goodfellow family have been at Hugbridge Farm since at least 1760; I've got an old tenancy agreement. It was part of the Harrington Estate, owned by Lord Harrington of Gawsworth Hall. In 1920 it was all sold up, 8,000 acres, all the farms, cottages, the flour mills at Bosley and the pubs. It took two days by public auction at Macclesfield Town Hall. The farms had been offered to the tenants and if they hadn't agreed a price, they'd gone to auction. So Hugbridge with 72 acres was bought for £3,000.

I was the youngest by 8 years of 4 brothers; father was the youngest of 10, grandfather was one of 9 and great-grandfather one of 14. My mother was Florence Cotterill from Broad Moss. She was a pupil teacher at Rushton School, then she met father and left teaching. Mr Banks was my Godfather, he was good friends with my father; but he didn't favour me in school. When he was elderly, he said, *"I don't want you to wait till I'm dead before I give you something; I'll give you £100 now for your benefit, while I'm still alive."* That was a lot of money then in the late 1950s.

I remember in the '40s and '50s, what a lot of corncrakes there were in the meadows, you heard them. We were making hay in July and August then and I think as haymaking became earlier and then silaging came in, that led to their demise.

A local character I remember was Ernest Robinson from Weathercock at Heaton. He worked on the farm and did decorating jobs as well. It was said that at Broad Moss, he painted the bedroom around Mrs Gaskill as she lay in her bed, even standing on it to paint the ceiling. He liked a drink and he would be the first customer at the Knot, then call in to the Oak before going home. He was once decorating at Hugbridge, around 1960 and decided to go with some friends to Manchester. He'd left his car there and came back drunk. They dropped him off and I said, *"You're not taking your car, I'll run you back."* So I took him up to Heaton and when we got there, he said to me, *"I'll run YOU back."* So I took the keys out - it had a starter on it which you pulled for ignition. He was pulling away at it and I couldn't get him out; I had to fetch his brother-in-law, so that we could manhandle him out and in to the house.

Rushton Fête fancy dress, 1950s.

Dales and Gibsons punting on the Feeder.

The Feeder Side, Rushton.

Dales and Gibsons - the 'Hanging Gate' gang.

Maypole Reunion in the 1970s, at the Methodist Chapel garden party.

Frank Brown

My father was Moses Brown, he was always known as Mo. Mum was Mary Shufflebottom, from Biddulph Park. We originally lived at Wall Hill Cottage; then we moved to Little Haddon Farm on the way to Wormhill, from 1943 to1954. Then we moved to Weathercock Farm at Heaton. Dad was a farmer and handyman; did a bit of building and joinery and he used to go round killing pigs. He'd got a humane killer and he used to walk, go one day, kill the pig, hang it and dress it, then go the next day and cut it up. He'd go 3 or 4 miles, say as far as Meerbrook or Bosley. I used to go with him sometimes. I was about 10 and thought it was a gruesome process, but you got used to it. They got me to fetch and carry, or spread some more straw on the floor, you had to try and keep the place clean.

Most people put water in the old wash boiler and got stoked up ready, and most had a pig bench or the equivalent about 6 feet long on 4 legs. Then first you had to catch your pig and put a rope with a slip knot round his top jaw. The art was to kill the pig and before it fell on the floor, lift it on the bench. Some were 20 score (20 x 20lbs), so it wasn't easy. You could hold 'em by th'ears. There were more men on farms then, you'd perhaps have 2 or 3; flirt it on the bench, then start pouring the hot water on; leave it 15 or 20 seconds to scald the flesh enough to be able to get the bristles off. You had to scrape away, starting at the nose end and go round to the tail and legs, then turn him over and do the same again. There was a knack to it; people who did it regular were much better at it. You had to really dig the scrapers in. Then you hung it up and cut it open and took the guts out and sorted them all out. You got the long intestine and put it on the end of a tap or hosepipe, then spread it all out and washed it through, then wrapped it up like you would a rope, twisting the last bit round. Dad had a market for them; I think it was Gilbert's at Cheddleton, they'd go for sausage skins.

The carcase was lifted up on a cambrill, usually a piece of oak with steps on to pull the pigs legs apart so you could cut it in half. We did this big pig for a man one day in an out-building where there was a beam to hang it on. The cambrill must have been a bit worm eaten and we'd just about got the pig up when it cracked in half and the carcase fell to the floor. Dad had to rig one up with a piece of metal pipe and after that, he took his own. He had a flat bag with two handles to carry his tools in. There were two scrapers, like hoes with a short handle and a hook on the back to pull the claws off the feet.

When we went on the train to Leek, you went through an archway to the ticket office and platform and I always remember passing Mr Collins' coalyard. It was opposite the Knot. He was always there, either waiting for customers or filling bags of coal. There was a little wooden hut and we thought he lived and slept there. He was an Irishman and about 1948 he went and everything disappeared.

When we lived at Haddon, we sometimes got off the bus from Leek at the Hanging Gate, a stop early; I don't know if it was to save a penny. Opposite was Arnold Turnock's yard. The shed was three storeys; the top level was joinery and below was sawing and storage. Vic Buckley was always in making a coffin and mum always stopped to pass the time of day. She was a bit nosy and always asked who it was for and he would reply, *"I think it's somebody from Leek."* He never liked to let on. One day Mrs Barker from Glen Le Side got off with us and says to Vic, *"You'll make mine when th' time comes, will you?"* He didn't know what to say. *"Alright." "I want it made comfortable; I don't want any splinters in my arse!"*

During the war, Dad was in the Observer Corps; they had posts on a grid system about twenty miles apart, covering most of England. The national headquarters were in Derby, and all sightings and hearings of enemy planes had to be reported immediately by telephone so that their direction and speed could be plotted. Our area was at an important junction for the Luftwaffe bombers intending to bomb Liverpool or Manchester. They would fly due west from the Wash until they could see Rudyard Lake and Bosley reservoir. They would then turn north or north-west depending on which was their target. The observers had to listen and could usually tell which city the bombers were heading for and therefore warn the anti-aircraft gunners of their approach. Dad was on duty one morning when a German reconnaissance plane flew over so low that he could see the pilot. This was quickly reported to HQ and the post was then issued with two rifles! At the end of the war, the observers and their wives were given a party at the Station Hotel (now the Knot) and were presented with gifts by the RAF area C.O. Group Captain Fielding. I still have the blue and white tea set featuring the Royal Observer Corps motif, which was presented to my father.

Arthur Needham, Home guard.

There were about thirty men in the home guard, which used to meet in a large room above the Station Hotel. Their CO was Mr Cartwright who had been an officer in the first war. Their training took place in the little valley between the old road and Charles Knowle lane. At the top end of the valley there is a small cliff against which they set up their targets for gunnery practice. They also had dugouts on the top of the hill nearby, from which they could see the entire bottom of the village and about a mile of the railway track.

A story that I remember being told was that there were no licensing hours before the first war; they were brought in then to aid war production. When the war ended, they had one day when there were no licensing hours. At the Golden Lion the landlord said whoever drank the most didn't need to pay for their ale. When it was totted up at the end of the day, Bill Mountford had drunk 27 pints and still managed to leave the pub on his feet.

I was a postman for 19 years. There was a man lived on Dingle lane who had been burgled, so he got this very savage dog, a big Alsatian. It had come from the police; they couldn't do any good with it. One day, I was walking round, I'd got my post bag and it had broken loose and attacked me. I managed to save myself by holding the bag in front of me and it was biting that. Another time, I was in the car and it was loose and I'd only got the letters. It came round the corner at me; I'd backed between two conifers and held the letters in front of me. As it bit them, I automatically struck it with my fist as hard as I could and managed to knock it unconscious. It was like punching a brick wall; my arm ached for a fortnight after.

R.O.C. Dinner, Knot Hotel, 1945.

Eva Chadwick

I lived at Sunnybank from when I was four; before that we lived in Heaton village, next to the Black Horse. Before the war, the only people to have a car there were Mr and Mrs L`Orange, who had a cottage next to the smithy. They were teachers from Stockport and came for weekends and holidays.

My sister, Gladys, married Ivan Nixon, the water bailiff and they lived at Feeder Cottage. It always seemed cold when we went down there to visit; the only heating was a range. Ivan had a bike and also a donkey and cart which they used to cart coal and stuff from Thompson Bridge, and feed for the few stock which they kept. He used to come up to Sunnybank with it too, when they had the last baby; he brought the washing up in the cart for my mother, to help out because Gladys had four other children not much older.

Mr and Mrs Meredith Dale.

I remember a bomb dropping below Thompson Bridge; it cracked a window at Sunnybank and I think it blew some out at Barleyford. We went to look at the crater afterwards, you can see it still.

Along the Feeder Side.

At Wolfdale in the 1940s. The tractor is a converted Dodge lorry. Cousins from Rhodesia, Alistair Ewing and John Simpson.

Jim Goodfellow with Una and Joe Cantrill.

Bill Wilshaw and Ralph Steele potato picking.

Hannah Twigg, Frank Brown, Gerald Robinson, Michael Fowler, Rev. Atkinson, Mr Banks, Muriel Malkin.

Mary Turnock

My father, Arnold, was a Rushton man, born in 1901. Mother was Mary Salt, born at Butterton, then lived at Onecote till she was four, when her father died. So her mother had to go and work in the Leek mills and she went to stay with her aunt and uncle near to Flash. They had two older children, so she was the poor relation and it must have been very hard for her at times.

Mum at Taylors Green, Dunwood, late 1930s.

Father had four older half brothers and sisters, James, John, Rosa and Mabel and a younger sister, May. Rosa and Mabel were in service. Sometimes Aunty Rosa would cycle home and bring her pet in the basket. Usually she came by train; she would send a postcard to my father, *"I'm coming on the 5 o'clock train on Saturday. Meet me at the station. Also tell dad to get the fiddle tuned."* Both my grandfather and Aunty Rosa played the violin. Grandfather made his own violin and during the war, when several members of the local band had gone to war, he played his violin for the walking Sundays. He was a trustee and the choirmaster at chapel and both James and John played in the band. Both my father and Aunty May were organists at Rushton Chapel and now I continue the tradition - a musical family!

My grandfather was a wheelwright and undertaker. He did a funeral, the weather was very bad and he caught pneumonia and died. My father was left to carry on the business, he was only 19. At this time they lived at Primrose, Heaton. One day, he was walking up the Marsh and stopped to talk to Mr Chappell, who suggested he built a house at the end of the garden. The ground was bought and Arncliffe was built, using a similar pattern as four other houses father had built in the village. No one wanted to buy it, so his mother bought it and the family moved down into the village.

My father had bought the workshop, which also consisted of a shippon, smithy and three fields; it had belonged to the Hanging Gate, and the business moved there; while sand,

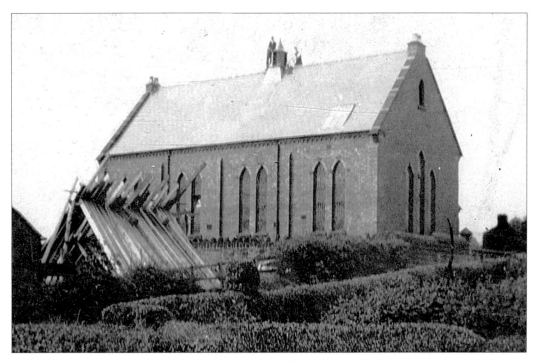

Men working on the Chapel roof.

Arnold Turnock, centre and Tom Cope, right.

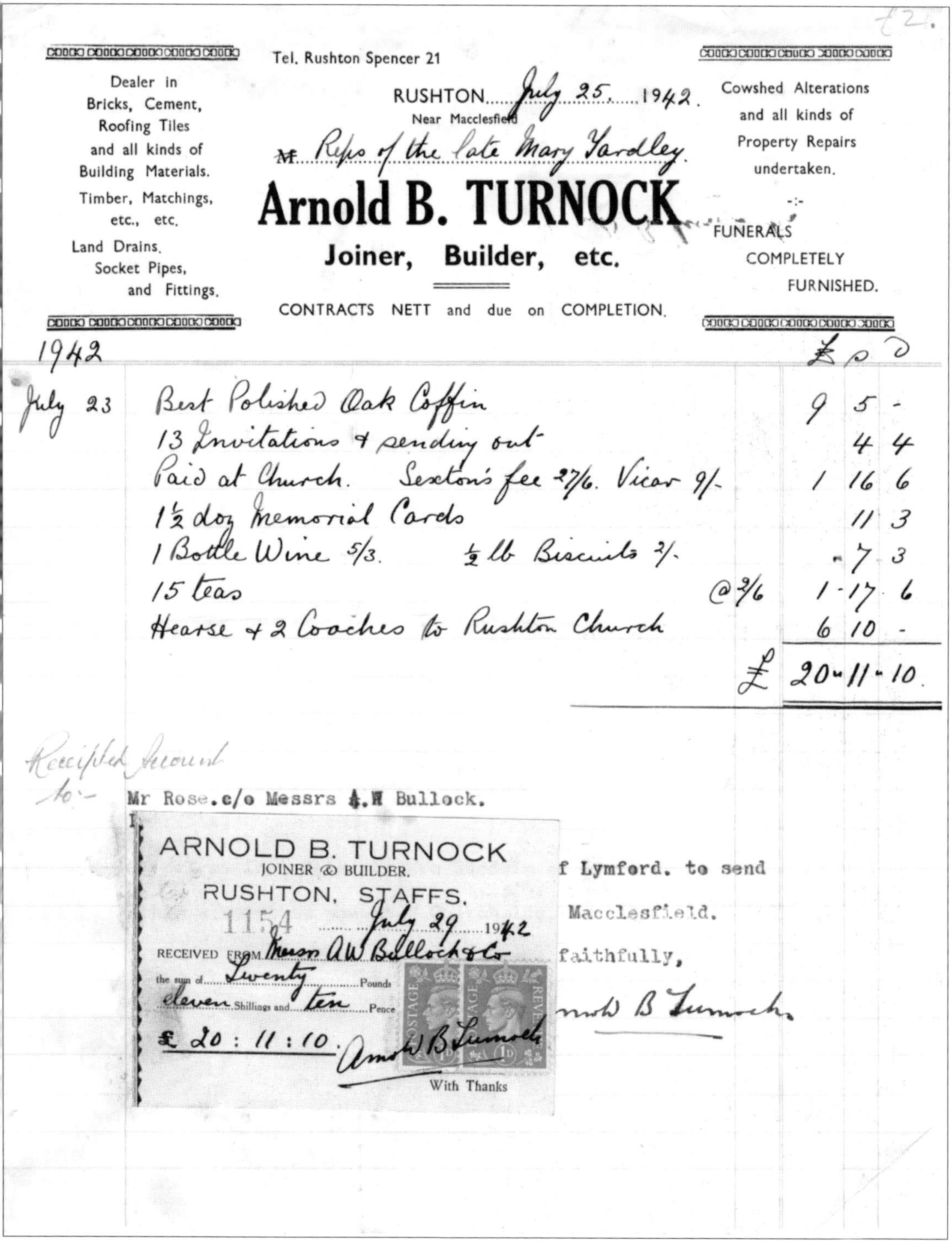

£2.

Tel. Rushton Spencer 21

RUSHTON. *July 25* 1942.
Near Macclesfield

M̃ *Reps of the late Mary Yardley.*

Arnold B. TURNOCK

Joiner, Builder, etc.

CONTRACTS NETT and due on COMPLETION.

Dealer in
Bricks, Cement,
Roofing Tiles
and all kinds of
Building Materials.
Timber, Matchings,
etc., etc.
Land Drains.
Socket Pipes,
and Fittings.

Cowshed Alterations
and all kinds of
Property Repairs
undertaken.

FUNERALS
COMPLETELY
FURNISHED.

1942		£	s	d
July 23	Best Polished Oak Coffin	9	5	-
	13 Invitations & sending out		4	4
	Paid at Church. Sexton's fee 2/6. Vicar 9/-	1	16	6
	1½ doz Memorial Cards		11	3
	1 Bottle Wine 5/3. ½ lb Biscuits 2/.	-	7	3
	15 teas @ 2/6	1	17	6
	Hearse + 2 Coaches to Rushton Church	6	10	-
	£	20	11	10

Receipted Account
to :-

Mr Rose. c/o Messrs A.W Bullock.

ARNOLD B. TURNOCK
JOINER & BUILDER.
RUSHTON, STAFFS.
1154 ..... July 29 1942
RECEIVED FROM Messrs A W Bullock & Co
the sum of Twenty ..... Pounds
eleven Shillings and ten Pence
£ 20 : 11 : 10   Arnold B Turnock
With Thanks

f Lymford. to send

Macclesfield.

faithfully,

nold B Turnock.

cement, lime and land drain pipes were stored at Arncliffe.

During the war, my grandmother had 2 evacuees, George and Elsie Ellis. George liked Rushton so much, he stayed until he left school and he still comes back to visit. Grandmother died in 1945 before my parents married.

Mother helped in the business, serving customers and also helping father. They once went to put up a hayshed on a farm at Sutton, following a gale, when several haysheds had been blown down. The farmer said, *"My shed won't blow down, because a woman helped to build it."*

When someone died, father went out to them and laid them out. If I was with him, I was taken along but I didn't like it. He'd say, *"There's nothing to be frightened of, the dead can't hurt you."* Then he came back and marked the coffin out for Vic Buckley to make, and then came and cut the material the right length for mother to make up.

As a child, I was often in the workshop when they were making coffins. I helped stain and polish them and helped mother to line them. We had rolls of material which were cut and nailed to the coffin. Then we put wadding on top, they told me it was to make them nice and comfy. I used to get all over hair off it. Then you turned it all inside. Mother used to make the cushions on the machine and I helped to stuff them and nail them on. The only thing he sent away for was the metal name plate and handles; we picked the parcel up from the station. When Rushton station closed, I was sent to Macclesfield on the bus to pick it up and catch the next bus back.

In the winter of 1947, someone died at the Eagle and Child at Gradbach and he had to walk there to lay them out and make the arrangements; he was gone most of the night. He used to hire a hearse and funeral car, but on this occasion they wouldn't turn out. Jack Wright from Leek offered to do the job, he was prepared to drive as far as possible and then walk the rest of the way to carry the coffin. From then on, father continued to hire from him until he retired and then from Norman Smith.

When father was 65 in the December, he started to wind the business down and had a sale in the following March, but he never really retired; he died suddenly in April having carried out his last funeral the week before he died.

Dad in the workshop at Primrose.

In 1980, we hadn't got a preacher one night and the minister suggested a Songs of Praise. The ladies sang a couple of items and the ladies choir was born from that. Three or four years later, Mr Charles Dale said, *"Will you let the men join you, we could make a mixed choir."* Which we did. After he died, it was named The Dale Singers, and we're still going.

Swythamley School 1963, Mr Stevenson's leaving party.

Swythamley School children at Swythamley Church in 1965, with Miss Doreen Brown.

Rushton School. Mr John Hyde, headmaster late 1950s.

Rushton School. Miss Dale's class 1963.
Back: - -, Ian Lovatt, Barbara Goodfellow, Paul Robinson, Mary Moss, - -, Patricia Allen, John Zuralew
2nd Dawn Robinson, Margaret Goodfellow, Peter Kennerley, Peter Nash, Mark Bradley, Cynthia Goodfellow, Doreen Eard
Front: Georgina Faulkner, Karen Edwards, Dorothy Knowles, - -, - -, Ian Eardley, - -, - -.

John Cook

Research that our family has done shows that the Cook or Cooke ancestors were at Onecote in the 1600s and Weatherworth, Bradnop in the early 1800s. From there, James Cook moved to Rushton in the 1840s to become a silk dyer, later being joined by William Cook, his nephew. Tradition has it that they were given a secret Chinese formula for the manufacture of a black dye which gave a special sheen when applied to silk, from a traveller on the highway down on his luck.

In 1865, William married Harriet Woodward and a large family soon developed. His eldest son, my grandfather, John, was born in 1866 and went on to run the corn mill in parallel with the dye business. The dye trade then would be more profitable because there was a great depression in agriculture due to five poor harvests and the dumping of grain from the Middle West of America, which made many farmers bankrupt.

At that time, a tall brick chimney had been constructed and a large wooden vat to steam the ingredients to the very high heat that was essential. Water was needed for milling the corn and for the copperas for the dye. The copperas came to Rushton station in trucks from a Welsh mine at Pontardulas. The vitriol and ammonia were supplied by horse and cart in carboys from Tennants of Cheetham, Manchester. The ingredients were put into the vat and it took three days to process the liquor. This was then taken in wooden barrels by horse and cart

to Upperhulme, Bollington and Leek. In its heyday, about 100 people worked there; it was said that the Golden Lion was built as a refreshment house for the workers.

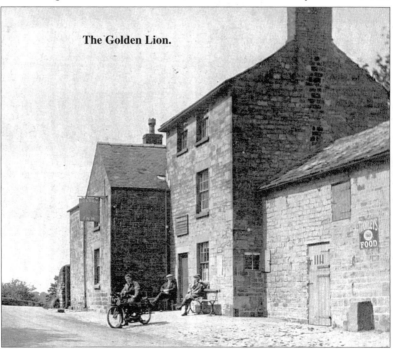

The Golden Lion.

Two of William's children died in infancy, two died very young of scarlet fever and his wife died shortly after childbirth, leaving five under the age of ten to be cared for. Tradition has it that William went to pieces, took to drinking and didn't survive many years after.

My father, John, and Uncle Bert, carried on at the dyehouse mill; I can just remember the water-wheel up there, and the carboys being delivered and Uncle Bert with his little wagon taking them out to the silk mills at Macclesfield, Bollington, Leek or Cheadle.

Eventually, they separated, Uncle Bert stayed there and father came up to this mill in

The Mill Pond.

Above:
The Cook family at the
Dyehouse, around 1930.

The workers in the 1950s.
Alf Holland, Tom
Sumner, Edna Robinson,
Mary --, Frank Bailey,
Derek Trueman, Les
Bailey, Jack Knight.

1936, which he bought off Mr Lockitt. He built this house, Brooklands, where I have spent my life. Uncle Bert carried on in a smaller way until he retired. The chimney had fallen in a storm in the 1940s. We've used the dyehouse as a corn store ever since.

I can only vaguely recollect the water-wheel going here, the mill pond was where the car park is now. If it ran dry, there was the Mill Pool behind the smithy, which was a backup. Father filled it with trout and people came and fished it. But unfortunately the garage next door once had a diesel leak, which got into the water and tainted the fish and people were complaining. So father said, *"Bugger this, we'll fill it in."* He started, but the council stopped him and it's been a weedy mess ever since.

We went onto an electric grinder when the wheel finished, the pool was drained and filled in because we hadn't enough room for the lorries which were coming in then. The early wagons were 30 cwts. From the dyehouse, a horse and cart took the corn out, Tom Sumner used to do that; then he took the wagon over, the first was around the beginning of the war. The corn came in 2 cwt railway bags on lorries from the docks at Liverpool. Some of the wheat came on the train and the milk lorries fetched corn back from Manchester on top of their churns.

About 1964, we had the first bulk wagon; that side has grown and grown. We employ about the same number of people now as then, but do business over a wider area.

At the old Leek market in town, we used to stand at the Coffee Tavern; most business was done there. I was about 19 when I was introduced to it. Besides that there was the Cock Inn on Derby Street, where they used to congregate. You'd get the reps and brokers from Manchester or Liverpool, selling bran or wheatfeed and the like. It was a hive of activity; I can remember father went into a little room there; 8 or 10 of them used to take it in turns to buy sandwiches. They had a drink or two and spent a couple of happy hours, doing business and relating jokes.

When the new market was built at Barnfields, we had an office down there until about 10 years ago.

Father also did a lot of business in pubs, a different pub every night of the week. He had a nap in the afternoon, so he could build his energy up for the night. Of course you could drink and drive then. He went to the Crag at Wildboarclough, the Robin Hood at Buglawton, the Queens at Bosley and all the local ones. He didn't always get home in one piece though.

In the blackout, he was in the Crown with Bill Bartram one night. He had a car identical with dad's. They were drinking till about two in the morning, both came out in the black dark, both got into the wrong car and didn't realise till the next morning what they'd done.

Dad.

On the Marsh.

Leek Market about 1920. Grandad, J. Cook on the left.

Ron and Mary Eyre

(Mary) I was 5 when my parents, Harry and Emily Sunter, bought the Transport Café and came to live in Rushton. Mum ran the café and dad went on the churn wagons, working for Bartram and Holland.

When I was 8 or 9, I can remember mum and dad used to go to the Oak on a Saturday night, playing nine-card Don or Crib. I was supposed to sit in the kitchen, but I used to hope that they hadn't enough people to make up a team, then I could go and play; I was good at cards.

(Ron) I came from Alton; I drove a lorry, taking sand or gravel from the quarries mainly to Manchester. So I used the road through Rushton and called in the transport café on a regular basis, chatting Mary up as a typical lorry driver does. We got married in 1955 and went to live in a converted railway carriage on the Cliffe Park side of the Lake. The two ends were built of brick. We put a generator in for lights and things. I used to start it up; it was in the garage, outside at the back, and I had a piece of string from it through the bedroom window, so when we were ready to jump into bed, I pulled this string and by the time I'd got in, it'd just about shut itself down.

A brook ran right past and we had some terrible floods; one morning I got up to see my slippers float off down the living room, it had come in. Eventually we sold it and moved down to the Marsh.

Before we got married, I'd had an accident. When stockcars first came to this country, I'd been racing them at Perry Bar, Birmingham till about 2am. Then gone home, took the lorry up to Hulland Gravel and put a load on by shovel; about 9 tons. I got as far as Butley Ash, the other side of Macclesfield, must have nodded off and crashed into a tree.

So I came off the road then and when the Robin Hood garage came up for sale we bought it. We ran a wagon, shifting aggregates for RMC; Dennis Eardley drove it and we bought a coach from Stoddards for £150, which I drove for a hobby to start with; it takes a while to build business up.

(Mary) After a while, we bought more coaches and gave the wagons up; and eventually the coaches took up so much time, we gave the garage up. We had our first brand new coach, a Bedford, in 1965; it cost less than £4,000 on the road. I drove small coaches,

Our first bus.

doing school and airport runs. When Painsley Catholic School at Cheadle first opened in the early sixties, we got the contract for two runs, one from Leek and one from Blackshaw Moor, that was the start of the school runs. Dennis has been with us for 48 years and retires this year. At the start, when we wanted to wash off the coaches, we had to use a stirrup pump in the brook by Bill Brassington's garage. There was no water in the village and no sewerage.

The time when Ron picked the first new coach up from Scarborough, he came straight back with it, picked up a school party from Broken Cross and took them to a village on the Austrian, Italian border. The day before they were due to start back, the snow on the mountains was melting very fast and it caused landslides which flattened the village. All you could see were bits of chimneys sticking up. There was only one way in and out, the bridge was down, so they were stranded there for several days until the army sorted things out. There was no communication, I just got a message to say, *"I'm stuck, the roads are washed away."*

(Ron) When we had the garage, Bernard Brown often came in. One day I said, *"Come on Bernard, let's go down the lake and have some fun."* So we got a 45 gallon oil drum, but we hadn't got a bung, so we borrowed one from Bill Brassington's garage next door. So we takes this down to the lake and both of us sit on it and off we go with two bits of wood for paddles. We get halfway across and it starts rolling, then Bernard starts worrying

about Bill's bung, *"We can't afford lose this, he'll go mad, Bill will."* It didn't matter if we got drowned as long as Bill's bung wasn't lost. We used to do all sorts of daft things; I couldn't swim, can't even now. We'd get a rowing boat out late at night, thinking of rowing down to Rudyard. Once the fog came down and we were lost. It was always with Bernard.

Our son, David, had a canoe and the Feeder ran behind our house, so I thought I'd have a go. I thought they were the same as a rowing boat, course the next thing is, it starts turning over; I went right under, couldn't swim and thought my day had come.

(Mary) There was only a foot of water, but so much noise. Arthur Chappell and Mary came out and Mrs Preston; it was so funny!

Bill Preston had a solid fuel central heating boiler in his workshop and when he stoked up, black soot came out. Ron used to wear a white shirt every day and there'd be a row of white shirts on the line covered in soot. One day, I lost my temper and Ron put a hosepipe down his chimney. Dennis Rimes, the policeman had to come out and calm us down. We've had some rows, but many laughs as well.

Bill Preston in the late 1960s.

Mrs Preston and David mid-60s.

Mid-1960s. Schoolchildren planting bulbs.

Fred Brown

My grandparents came here to Barnswood in 1925. The farm had been part of the Rudyard Estate, which was owned by the Earl of Macclesfield. It was offered for sale in 1919. The tenant then, Mr Fletcher, paid £150 a year. I would guess that he bought the farm then and when times got hard, had to sell to my grandparents.

They milked 30-35 cows. I remember dad saying about taking the milk down to the station. When we were haymaking and the steam trains were running, we had to watch the Bottom meadow, when the hay was about ready. You had to go down and watch for the 4 o' clock train coming through, the last train before you were hubbling it up and carting it. I've seen the fire from the cinders come up the bank and start to come up the field burning the hay.

When I was a child in the hayfield at dusk, you could hear nightjars up in the wood whirring away. If there was a peewit's nest in the field and you were muckspreading, you had to put a churn lid over it and then carry on - we carried one on the tractor. We always grew a few acres of greencrop and when you ploughed, you always marked the nest, so it wasn't damaged. I think crows and magpies and other vermin have done for them, they're not controlled nowadays. We used to shoot the wood above on a Wednesday night in summer. A group of us went through one time; we beat from this end right through and left three guns on the track and beat back again. We got 4 as we went and 3 coming back, 7 foxes in one night.

Dan Knight worked here. He farmed at Isle Farm on Gun. He milked his cows, then came down here with his little pony and cart. He learnt me to trap moles when I was 6 or 7 and I've done it ever since. I've done it for lots of people since I've retired; always with traps, never poison. One year, I caught over 150. I've caught 2 silver-grey ones and a sandy coloured one.

Going back to younger days, I can remember in wartime, going out of school one lunchtime and seeing the road full of American Army tankers parked up from Malkin's, all

The 'ice yacht', Ken and Cyril House.

across the Marsh and up the old road. There must have been half a mile of them; all the drivers were in the transport café.

We used to cycle to dances at Gawsworth, Eaton and Marton. The road would be full of lads and girls on bikes going and coming back. When the pylons were erected through Bosley and Rushton, I was at Bosley Youth club one night and Johnny Fairhurst and me had a bet to race up a pylon for ten bob. This was before they'd put the wire on. I won, I'd got to the top and he was only half way up; but he never paid me until some years later when we had a reunion at Smallwood and people were on to him to honour his bet, so he put a pound in my pocket later on, the bet with interest!

On frosty nights, if I was cycling towards Bosley I'd stop and listen to the trains. It used to take them ages to come up from Bosley station, past Morris Green, then the dyeworks towards Rushton. They might have 50-60 goods wagons on and start skidding; then blow sand on the rails and start off slowly chugging.

In 1963, when the lake was frozen and covered in snow, we put a bed with a counterpane over it on the middle of the lake for a prank. It was top secret, only 5 of us knew about it. It was reported in the Daily Express and other papers that it was a mystery object, car drivers stopped to stare; they thought someone had tried to use it as an ice yacht!

1976 was a very hot summer. In August, we used to meet down by the lake, Isobel Bailey, David Eyre, Victor, Bill Cheetham and one or two other locals. We had a boat and were swimming around. Bill says to me, *"You swim well, have a go across the lake."* So I said alright, if they went with me with the boat. So I swam right across, stood up and then swam back.

Tom Simpson, Sid Bailey, George Sherratt, Wilf Gibson.

Irene Gordon

I was born in 1932, near to the Hanging Gate Inn, and I believe I was bought into the world by Mrs Sumner, Tom's mother, who attended to births and deaths. My dad was Sam Lovatt and my mother, Annie Eardley from Thornyleigh. We moved up to Sugar Street, where my brother Stan and I spent most of our childhood.

Dad came from Biddulph Moor originally, having worked down Black Bull Pit; but when the general strike was on, he came to drive for Mr Moss and soon afterwards became a partner, so the business became Moss and Lovatt.

He used to take us with him in the car when he was looking for business and we'd go into people's farmhouses and dad would say to me, *"At jus goin' sing for 'em?"* I think he thought I might charm them; so I sang, *"Now Zacheus was a little man."* And I used to get a penny or sometimes a sixpenny bit.

After school, Stan and I had to fetch drinking water from Port o' Bella well; he had a big white bucket with a lid on and I had a little bucket, but there was not much left in mine by the time I got home. We used to take church magazines to Mrs Mycock's at Little Haddon and she would toddle off to the pantry, saying, *"Just a minute, I'll get yo an egg apace."* It was a lovely brown egg which we treasured.

We lived next door to Leonard Mason and we thought he must be very posh because he had a maid, Miss Moores, who wore a lovely starched apron and cap. She came from Bosley every day on the train.

When dad was on the milk lorry and it was the big churns, he'd come home and say, *"Av 'ad an argument with a churn an' eets bosted me toe!"* Then he'd cut the front off his boot, bandage it up and carry on.

Mother died young, I was only six and went to live with Grandma. Then dad

Mr Moss on the right.

remarried, to Olive Dakin, and I came back to Rushton. I went to Leek High school on the train; it was always full on Wednesdays because the marketeers from Manchester came with their bundles to set up stall in Leek. They carried them on their backs. We couldn't always get a seat that day.

During the war, dad was teaching Olive to drive and being a bit nervous, when she met a bus or big lorry, she'd say, *"What shall I do with this bus, Sam?"* and he'd reply, *"Send it a postcard, wench!"* So she'd have to carry on. And in the school holidays in wartime, she drove a milk lorry, so that the men could have a holiday, there being a shortage of drivers. The farmers used to turn the lorry round in the yard for her and load the churns; I used to go with her. One day the lorry was making a loud noise and she was scared to drive it, but father said, *"Keep goin', it'll get thee wom."* And it did.

Just after this, Geoff was born and a few years later, Mavis came along to complete the family. Many times during the war, when we were going to have breakfast, dad would go round the house banging a carving knife on a bucket and shouting, *"Pig, pig, pig!"* Then he'd come back with a chunk of bacon cut out of a side we'd had hanging up out of sight, because it was Black Market.

I used to work in Macclesfield and travel by train and every Friday, I took a basket with six dozen eggs, and one morning I was late and the train was waiting for me, when I slipped and fell on the wet sleepers in front of the engine on top of the eggs. The engine driver got down and helped me up and bundled me into the train with all the smashed eggs. Oh what a mess!

When I started going out with my future husband, Stan, dad would say, *"Is th' wageen mon cumin' t'nate?"* And they'd sit there all night talking about lorries. When we got married, dad said he wouldn't give me away; Stan had got to give him an ounce of Royal Seal tobacco in exchange. Stan said he'd got the best bargain, but dad said, *"Thee dusna know yet."* Who am I to judge?

Sam Moss, Sam Lovatt, Jack Cook.

Ann Dowley

My father Jim Dowley was born in 1917 at Smallthorne, then a smallish village on the edge of the Potteries. In 1945 he married Gladys Bowyer from Charles Knowle Farm, Rushton and on demobilisation from the Army the family came to live in Rushton.

From then his life was spent living and working in Rushton as he became one of the village postmen from 1946 until retirement in March 1980. In all that time I never knew him to have a day off work either through illness or due to the weather.

He'd leave Town Cottage and walk through the Churchyard to be at the Post Office for 6am six days a week. The mail was brought by van from Macclesfield and then sorted at Rushton. Dad's round was up one side of the Marsh and then into Heaton and over to Swythamley. Indeed some of the farms were actually in Meerbrook. Then he'd return from his last drop at Overhouses, a return trip of about 14 miles, all on foot. Always willing to lend a helping hand, he'd collect a pension or fetch a newspaper for someone.

It wasn't that long ago when we used to have a mail delivery on Christmas Day. My brother and I would be up very early that day opening presents before Dad went off to work. It was lovely to get cards and packages delivered on Christmas Day.

In the early days he wore clogs made to measure by a farmer on his round. When the weather was very wet he had to wear wellingtons. He didn't like day after day of wet weather. Mail bags then were made from rough canvas and took some drying out ready for the next day. Uniforms too were made from serge with just a cape for the rain. A hiker, meeting Dad one beautiful Spring morning, said he must have the best job in the world, to which Dad replied, *"The weather isn't always like this."*

Dad, 1970s.